masterpieces
of italian design

project editor VALERIA MANFERTO DE FABIANIS

editorial coordination GIADA FRANCIA

graphic design MARINELLA DEBERNARDI

text DESIGN.DOC

Con/tents

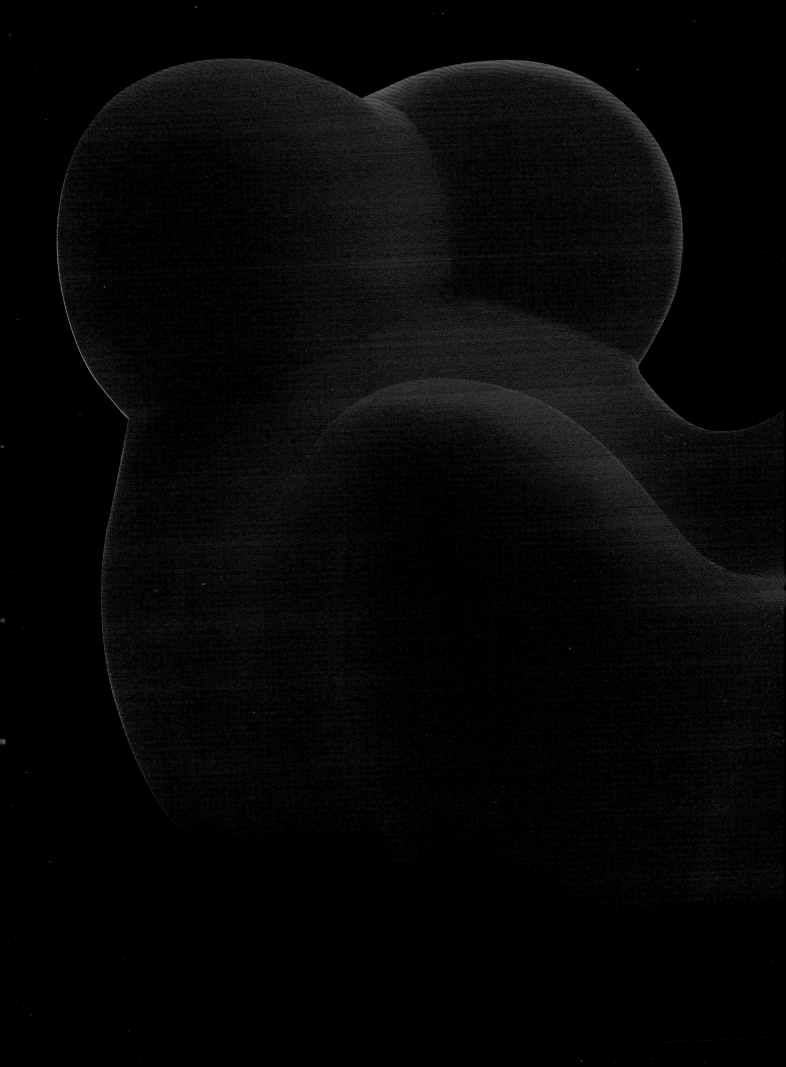

introduction

*M*ade in Italy tells the story of Italian industrial design as seen through the work of its protagonists: the designers, the creators of our material world. In the pages of this small book, we have gathered some of the best known design objects – chairs, tables, settees but also electrical appliances, books, switches . . . around their respective fathers, the designers. This is not quite a chronological history but a temporal-thematic one that highlights the main features of Italian design from its birth to the present day. Five chapters for five historical periods, plus a sixth dedicated to foreign designers, the ones adopted by Italian design: from its earliest beginnings, suspended between craftsmanship, early industry and art, up to the contemporaneity of today's news, without forgetting the masters and radical design, which is capable of adding new socio-political meaning even to creativity. A history told through the key figures, with schematic summaries describing their design approach, enriched by a selection of images of some of their most important products.

So here are the beginnings, when industrial design found its initial stimulus in the relationship between craftsmanship and early industry, with results that were both exercises in artistic expression and the first instances of mass production.

The post- Second World War masters of Italian design bear witness to the adoption of the rationalist paradigm by interpreting it through artistic inspiration with functionality. Italian creativity then goes on to pursue the radical experience where design is full of utopias and symbolism, manifestos and political declarations, together with post-modern visions that are in contrast with rationalist "prohibitionism." To reach today's reality (which, in part, will be that of tomorrow) that is no longer defined uniquely by Italian designers but also by numerous foreign designers, who find fertile ground for expression in Italy.

The choice of a precise schematic policy may appear to be somewhat discriminating (and we apologize for any omissions), but the style we have adopted is instrumental for reading and clarifying the complex, structured and constantly changing system of Italian design. This volume obviously does not claim to be comprehensive, it is just a small contribution – and not just in the metaphorical sense, due to its miniformat – in the narration of the kaleidoscopic world of Italian industrial design.

FORMA TEORIA
FORMA REALE

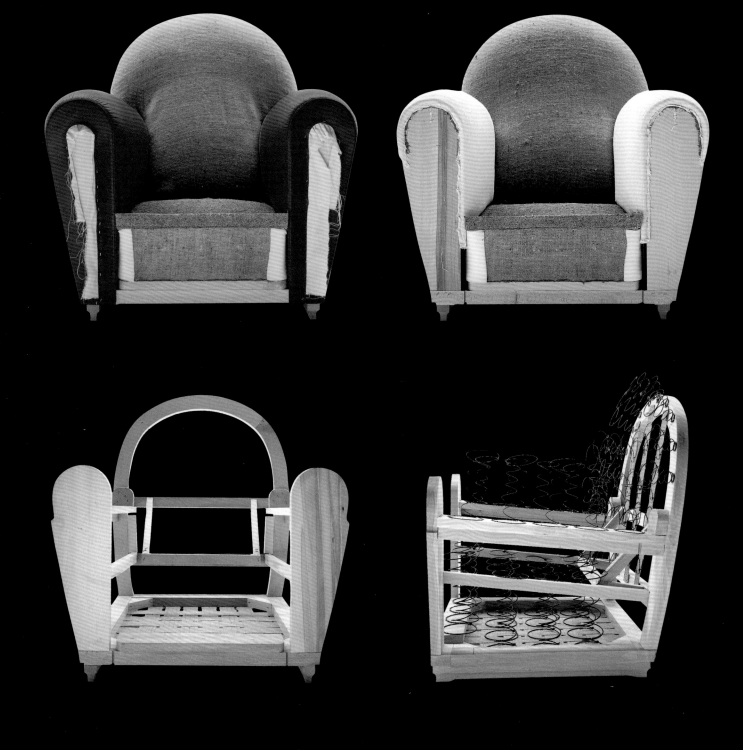

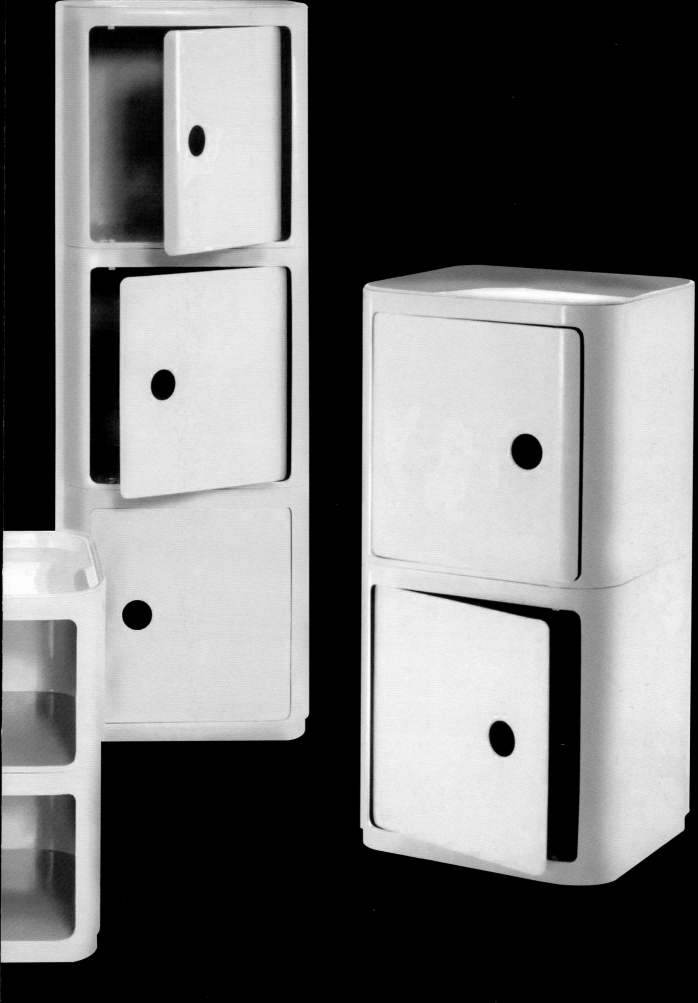

once upon a time . . .

20 Moka Coffee
Machine, 1937, Bialetti.

21 Follia Chair,
Giuseppe Terragni,
1934, Zanotta.

Italy is lagging behind in the industrialization process (apart from a few isolated cases such as those of ceramics and textile manufacturing), a process which would only become mature toward the end of the 20th century, concentrated mainly in the northern regions. It is an entrepreneurial activity coupled with the high end of the artisan tradition, drawing its characteristics from such a relationship.

It was on this hybrid terrain that the first artists and architects moved knowledgeably – the figure of the modern designer is still to come – distinguished by a transversal and eclectic approach to design, bearers of original stylistic expressions in line with the cultural debate of the time, also marked by a wide variety in taste.

On the one hand there was the Modernist movement with its rationalist anti-decorative doctrines, and on the other hand the persistence of historicism, as represented, for example, by Neoclassical nuances which remained both in architecture and in home furnishings. A bi-polarity which, not being resolved by either position taking the upper hand, generated, by fusion, the very beginnings of the original "Italian way."

Franco Albini

rchitect (Robbiate, Milan 1905-1977). Franco Albini participated in the Milan Triennial in 1933 and in 1936; his areas of interest are installations and interior decoration. He designed low-cost housing areas in line with the diktats of the Modern Movement of which he was the main Italian exponent. His decorative pieces demonstrate a personal and rigorous conception united with a rare technological and structural synthesis. He has lectured in Venice, Turin and Milan. He has received three Compasso d'Oro (Golden Compass) awards, an Olivetti award for architecture and the Royal Designer for Industry Award from the Royal Society of Arts in London.

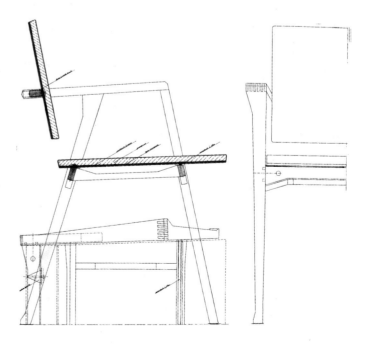

Luisa Chair, 1955, Poggi.

Fiorenza
Chair

1939, Arflex

Veliero Bookcase

1940, Poggi

Margherita Chair

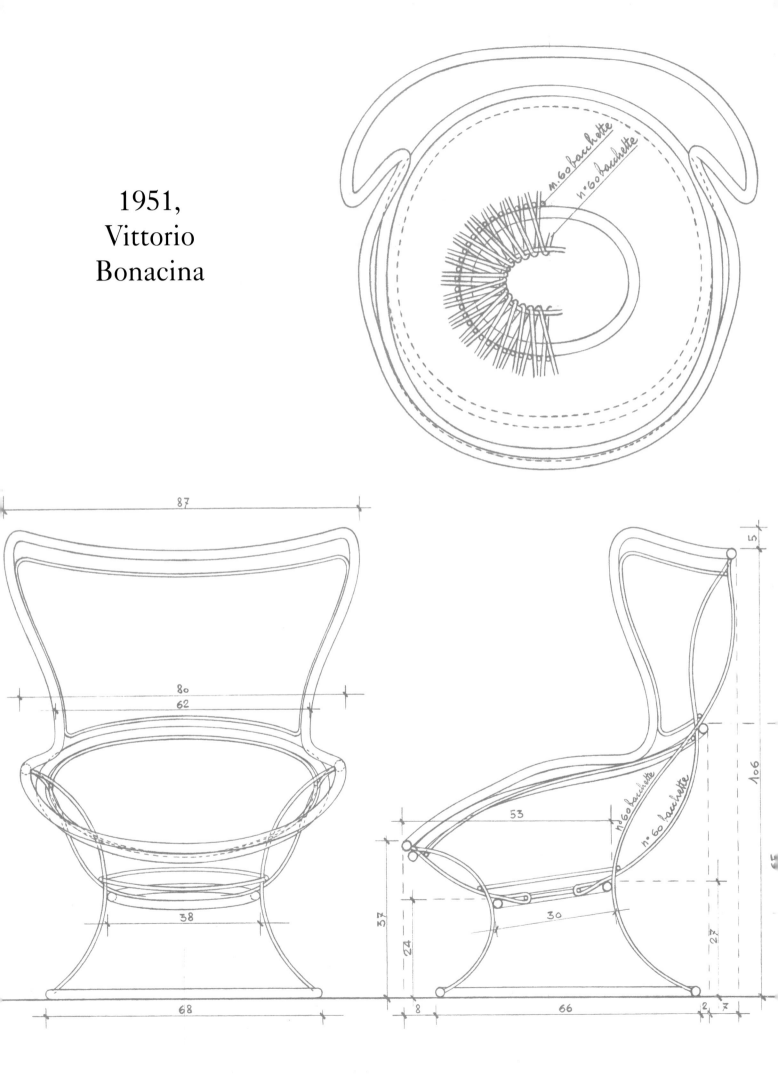

1951,
Vittorio
Bonacina

Carlo Mollino

rchitect (Turin, 1905-1973). Participated in and won many architectural competitions and designed various buildings which rejected rationalism and the precepts of the régime. In the 1940s he was involved in interior design and the design of objects, often with one-off pieces or limited editions, experimenting with new materials and techniques. With a restless and a multifaceted personality he explored various disciplines, leaving a large collection of books, periodicals, photographs, drawings and sketches.

Milo Mirror, inspired by the Miller House mirror, 1936, now Zanotta.

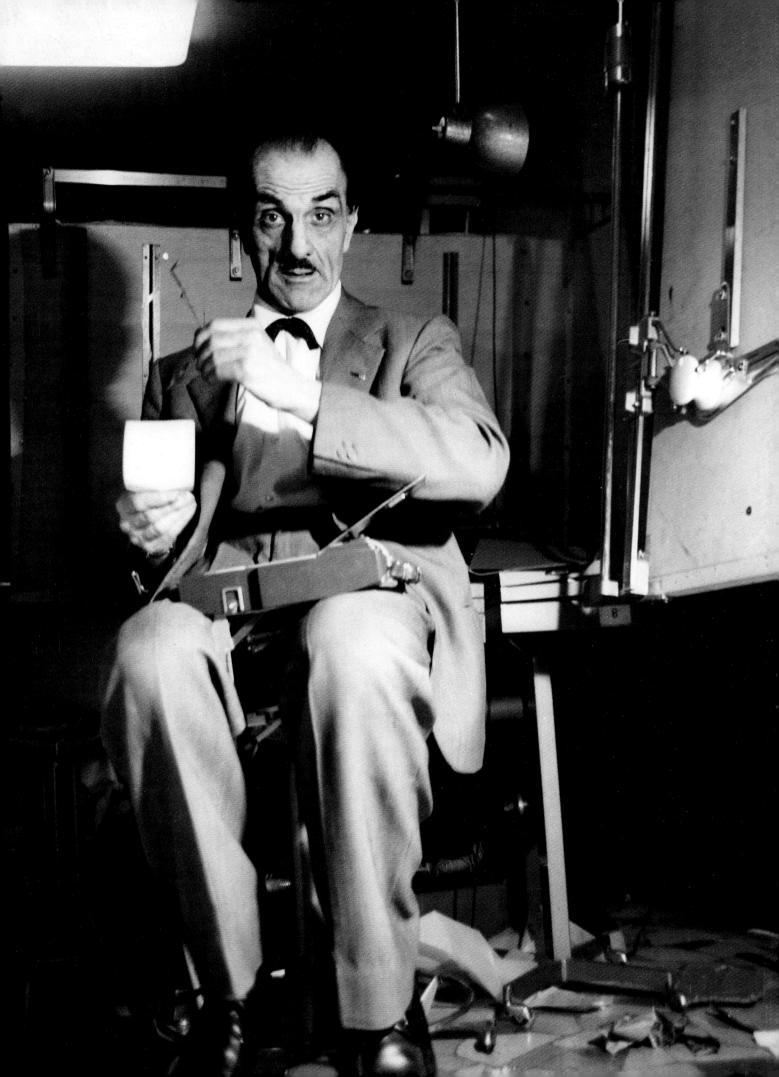

Coffee table in curved plywood,
1950, Bruno Bischofberger
Collection-Zurich

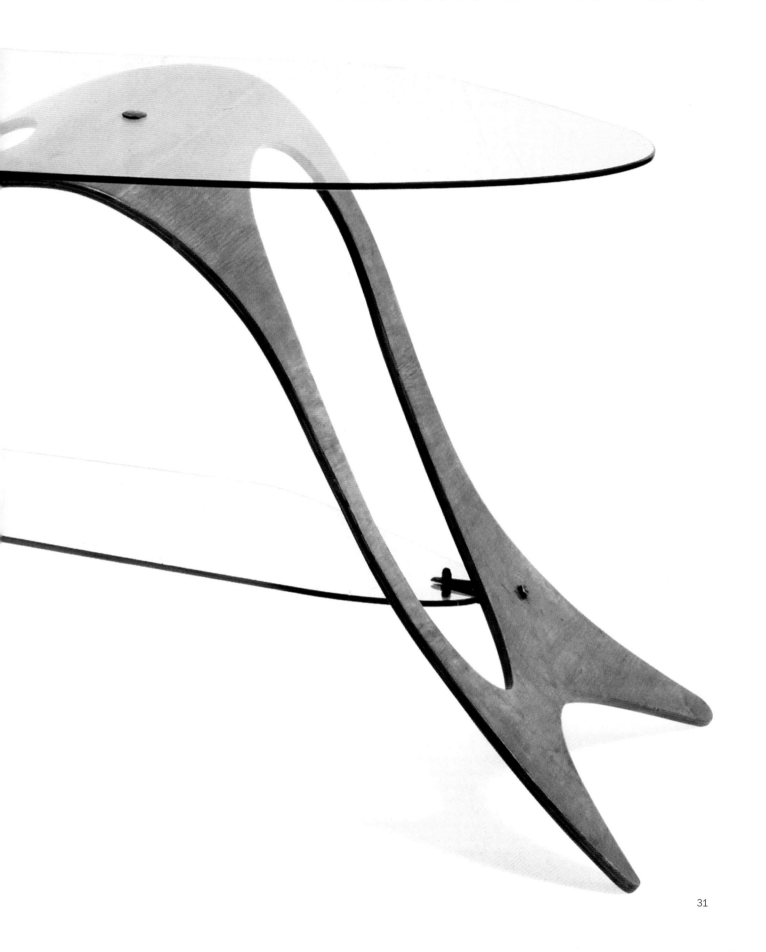

Prototype
Cutlery

1959
Reed & Burton

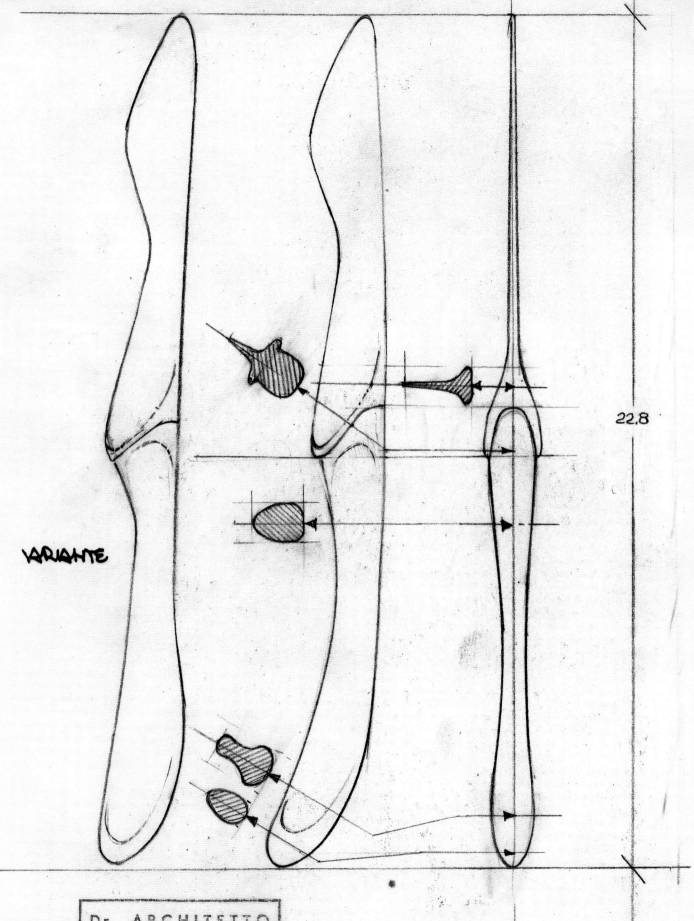

VARIANTE

22.8

Dr. ARCHITETTO
CARLO MOLLINO
VIA C. di PAMPARATO N. 9
TORINO - TELEF. 70.028

COLTELLO

Reed & Barton, concorso
dic, 59

Marcello Nizzoli

Artist (Boretto, 1887-1969, Camogli). Studied architecture, painting and decoration at the Institute of Art in Parma and then worked as a graphic designer in advertising and as an interior designer. He worked with Giuseppe Terragni and Edoardo Persico in interior design and installation projects. In the 1940s he worked for Olivetti, designing several famous products and winning three Compasso d'Oro awards, one of which was for the mythical Lettera 22 typewriter. Self-taught, he designed apartment blocks and office buildings, here again for Olivetti, and was awarded an honorary degree in Architecture from the Polytechnic in Milan in 1966.

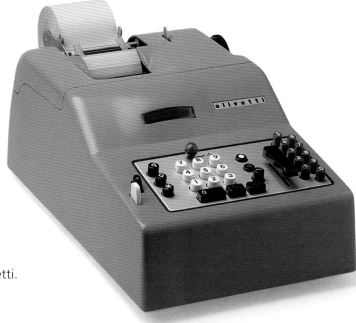

Divisumma 14 Calculator, 1948, Olivetti.

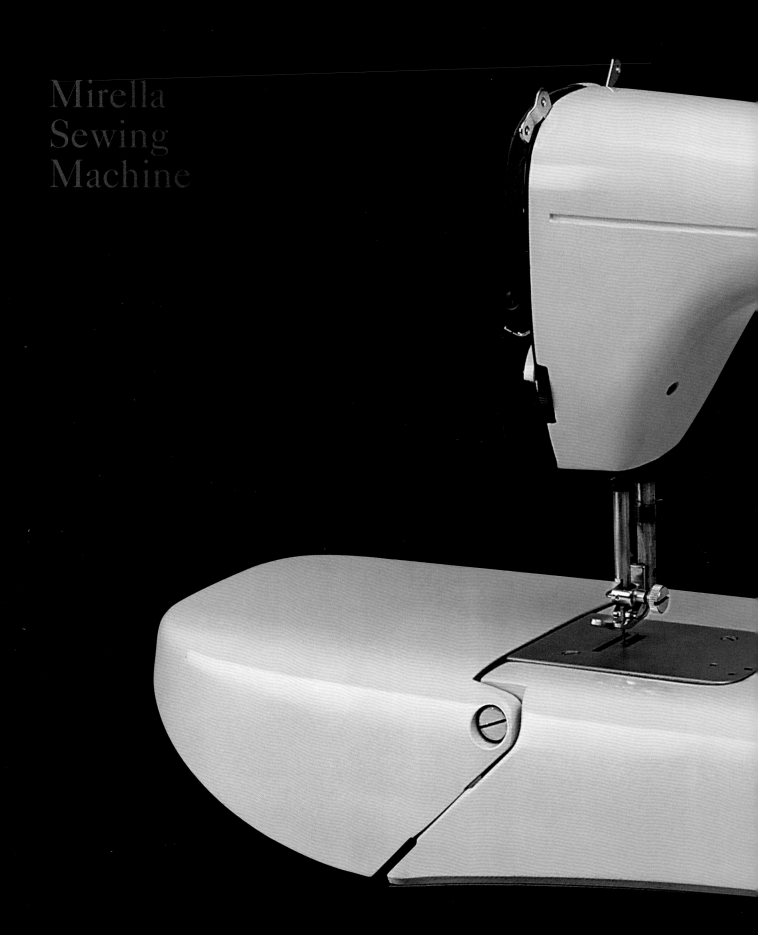

Mirella
Sewing
Machine

1957, Necchi

Lettera 22
Typewriter

Olivetti
from 1950 to 1963

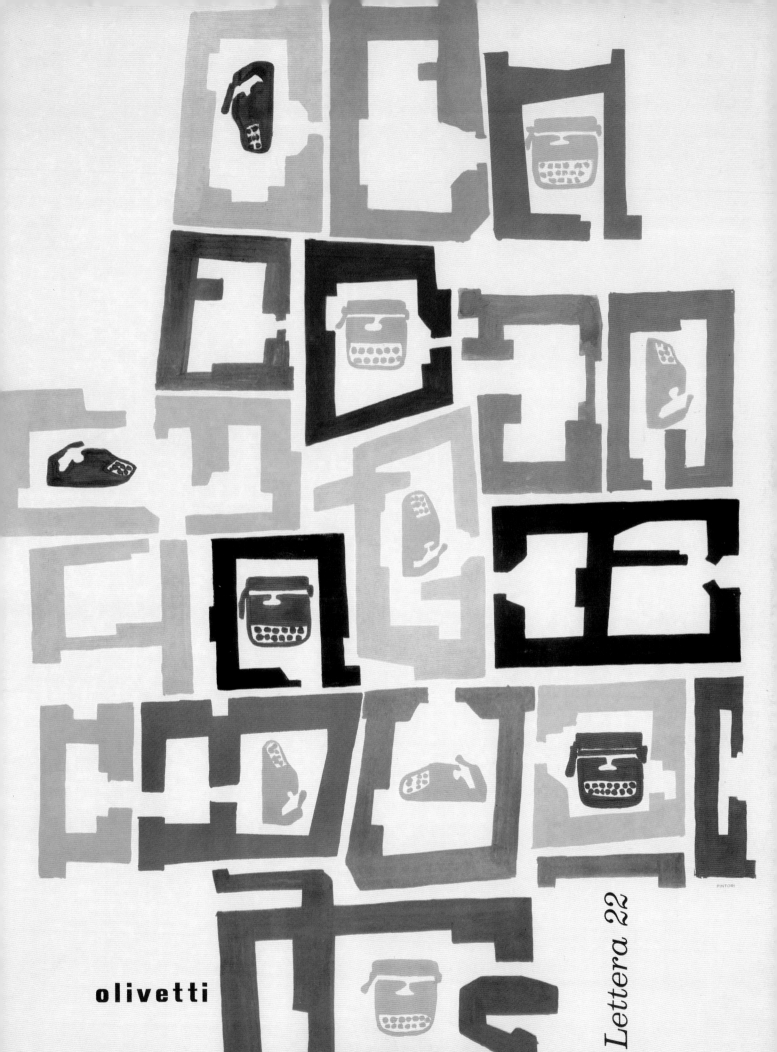

olivetti

Lettera 22

Gio
Ponti

Architect (Milan, 1891-1979). His creative multifaceted personality pushed him to work in different fields, from architecture to industrial design, from teaching to publishing, founding the magazines Domus and Stile. The Fifties was his most fertile period; in it he produced his most important works, distancing himself from the Neoclassical inspiration of his début (first and foremost the Pirelli skyscraper in Milan). He also designed theater and film sets, furniture, furnishings for transatlantic liners, lamps, objects and ceramics.

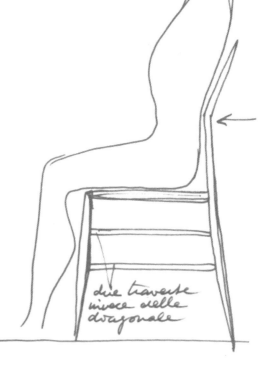

"Superleggera" (Super-lightweight) chair, 1957, Cassina.

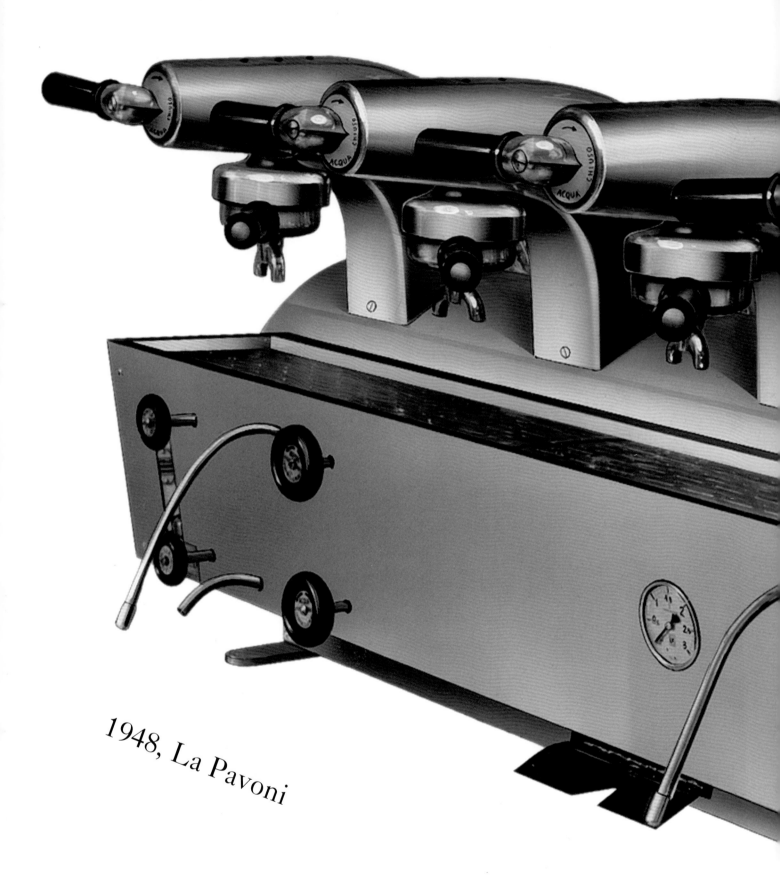

1948, La Pavoni

La Cornuta
Coffee Machine

Conca Cutlery

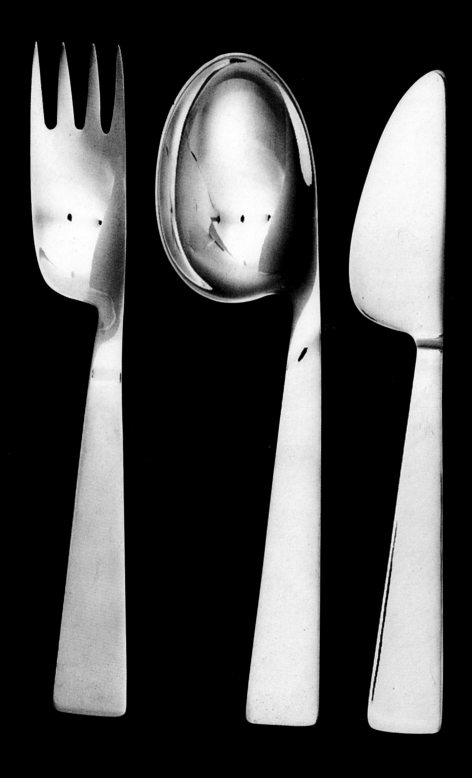

1951
Krupp Italiana

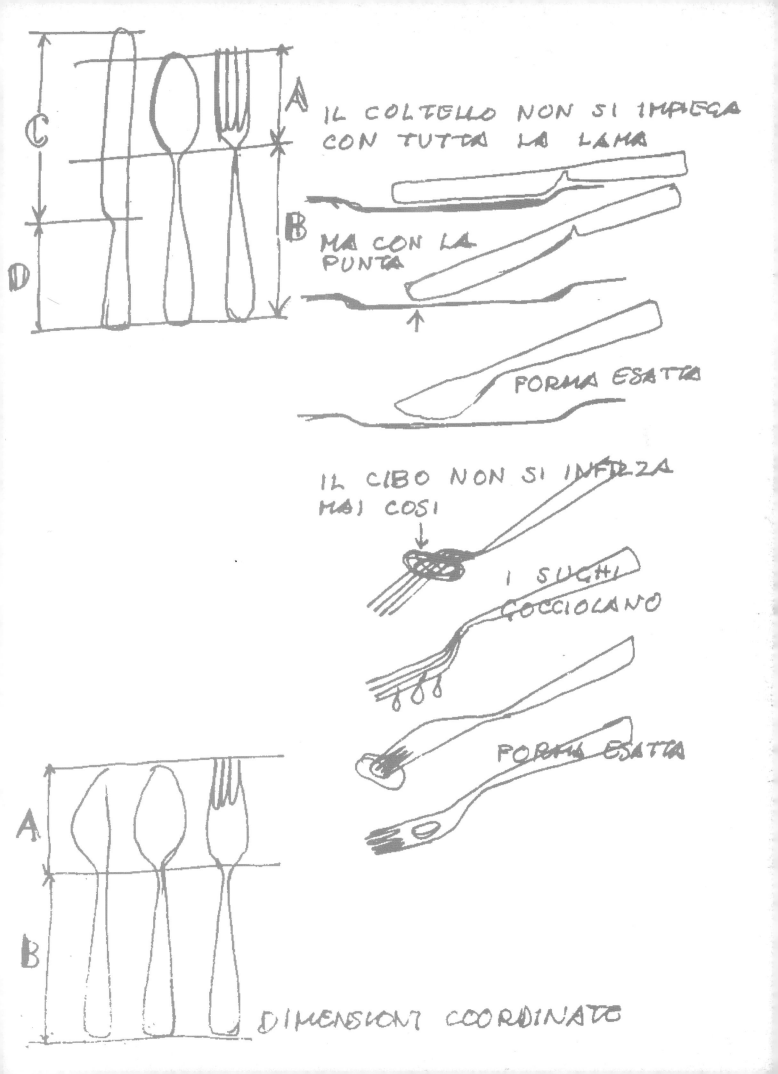

IL COLTELLO NON SI IMPIEGA CON TUTTA LA LAMA

MA CON LA PUNTA

FORMA ESATTA

IL CIBO NON SI INFILZA MAI COSI

I SUGHI GOCCIOLANO

FORMA ESATTA

DIMENSIONI COORDINATE

Handle / Lama

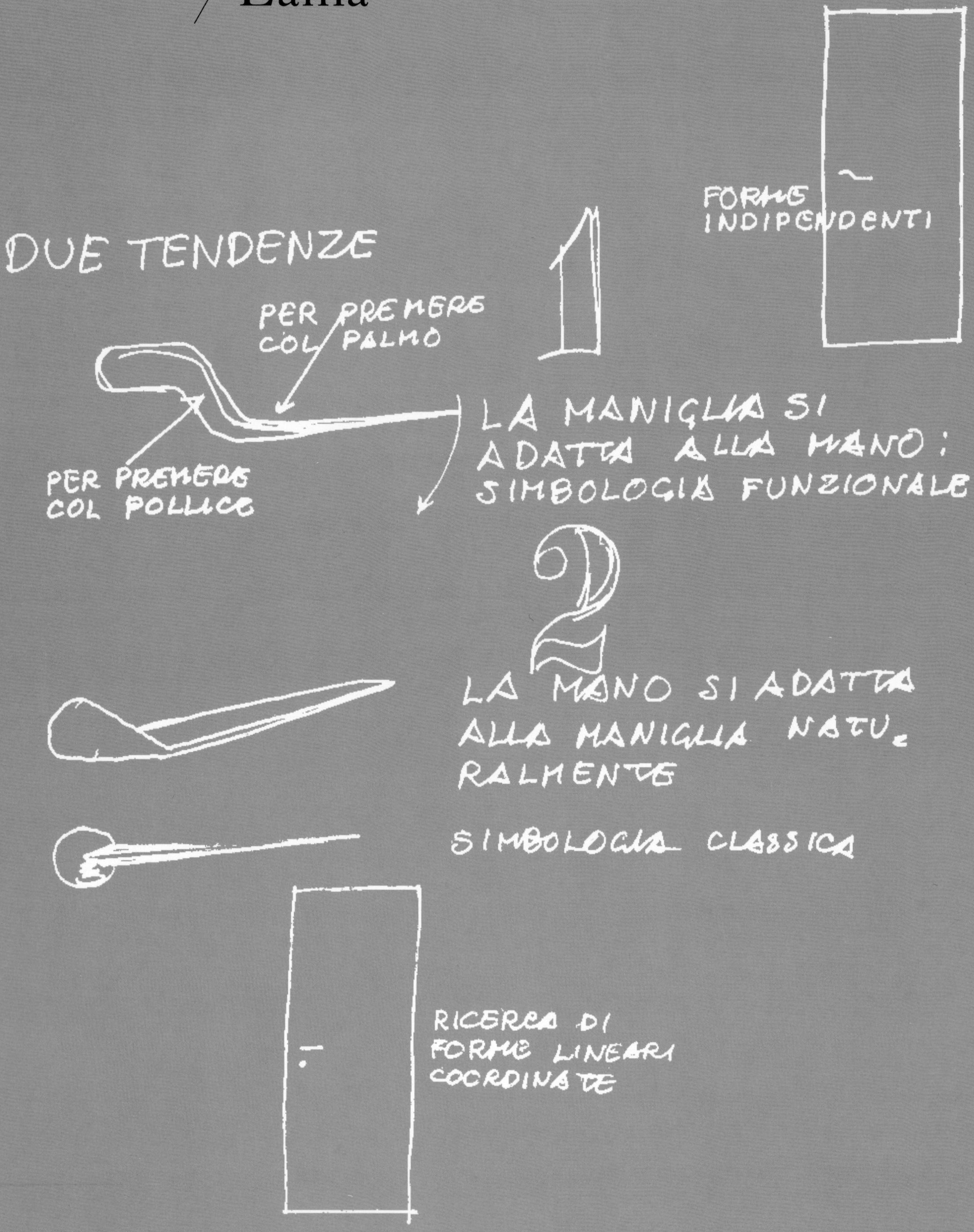

DUE TENDENZE

1

FORME INDIPENDENTI

PER PREMERE COL PALMO

PER PREMERE COL POLLICE

LA MANIGLIA SI ADATTA ALLA MANO: SIMBOLOGIA FUNZIONALE

2

LA MANO SI ADATTA ALLA MANIGLIA NATU-RALMENTE

SIMBOLOGIA CLASSICA

RICERCA DI FORME LINEARI COORDINATE

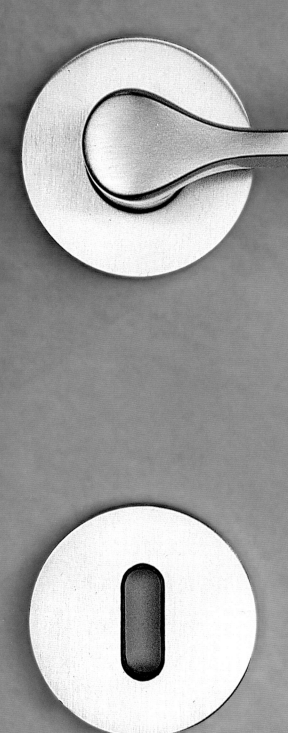

1957, Olivari

the masters

50 Giogali Chandelier,
Angelo Mangiarotti,
1967, Vetreria Vistosi.

51 top Caccia Cutlery,
Luigi Caccia Dominioni,
1938, Alessi.

51 bottom Fish Steamer,
Roberto Sambonet,
1957, Sambonet.

In the period after the Second World War, Italian industry was consolidated in the form which still today frames the originality of the productive system: a few large industries and a widespread network of small and medium sized companies, developed by the force of virtuous artisan experience. It was the period of large-scale construction of houses and furniture production, of building new apartments in the large industrial cities to cope with the waves of immigration from the south of Italy by those in search of work. It was the time of the appearance of new materials – plastics above all – and of innovative techniques. It was the moment of the Masters of Italian design, architects and designers who worked alongside thoughtful businessmen who were determined to give character to the new industrial products. Even today, they are still key figures, thanks to their activity which was not limited to design and research but included also cultural activities, activities aimed at production and consequent sale, and also the promotion of a widespread sense of aesthetic sensitivity: through exhibitions and events or the foundation of associations like the ADI (Association for Italian Design) in 1956 and awards like the Compasso d'Oro, founded in 1954.

Achille Castiglioni

Architect (Milan, 1918-2002), worked in the firm of his elder brothers, Livio and Pier Giacomo, on projects in the fields of town planning, architecture, exhibitions, displays and product design. In 1956 he was one of the founders of ADI (Association for Italian Design).

He and his brother Pier Giacomo designed objects and standard furniture for numerous companies, winning, between 1955 and 1979, seven Compasso d'Oro awards.

He was the pragmatic and ingenious creator of cult pieces in which synthesis was combined with innovative detail, independently of the styles and trends that alternated throughout his long career.

Parentesi Lamp, 1970, by Achille Castiglioni and Pio Manzù, Flos.

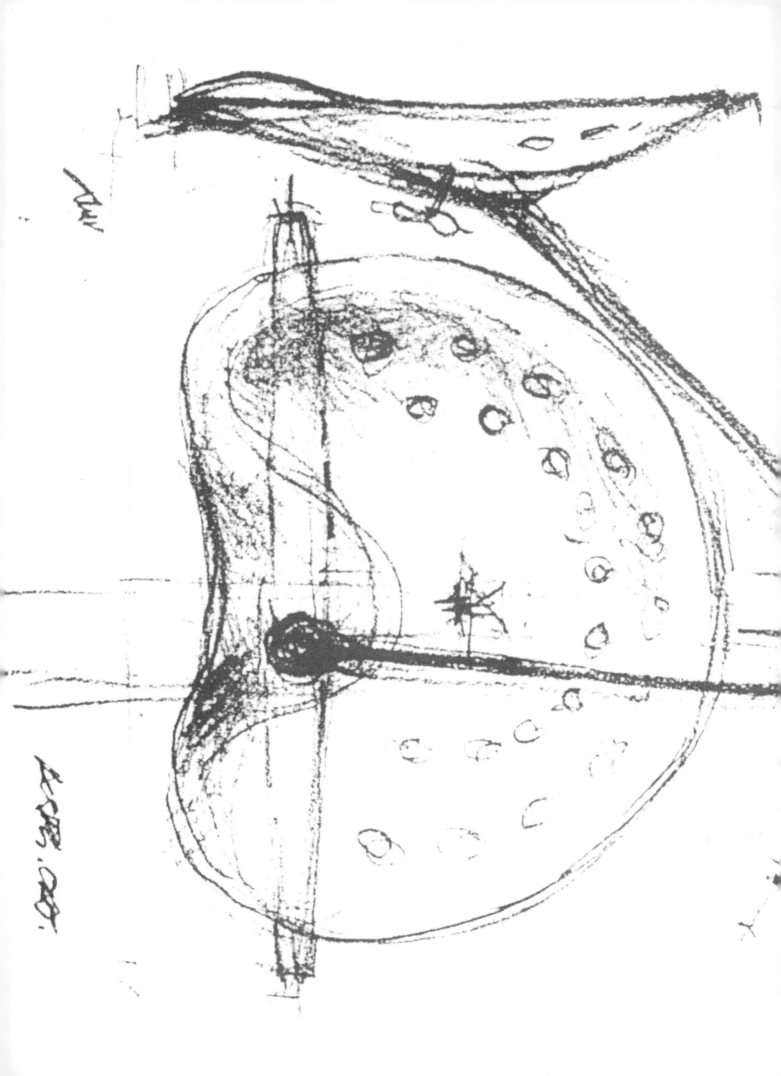

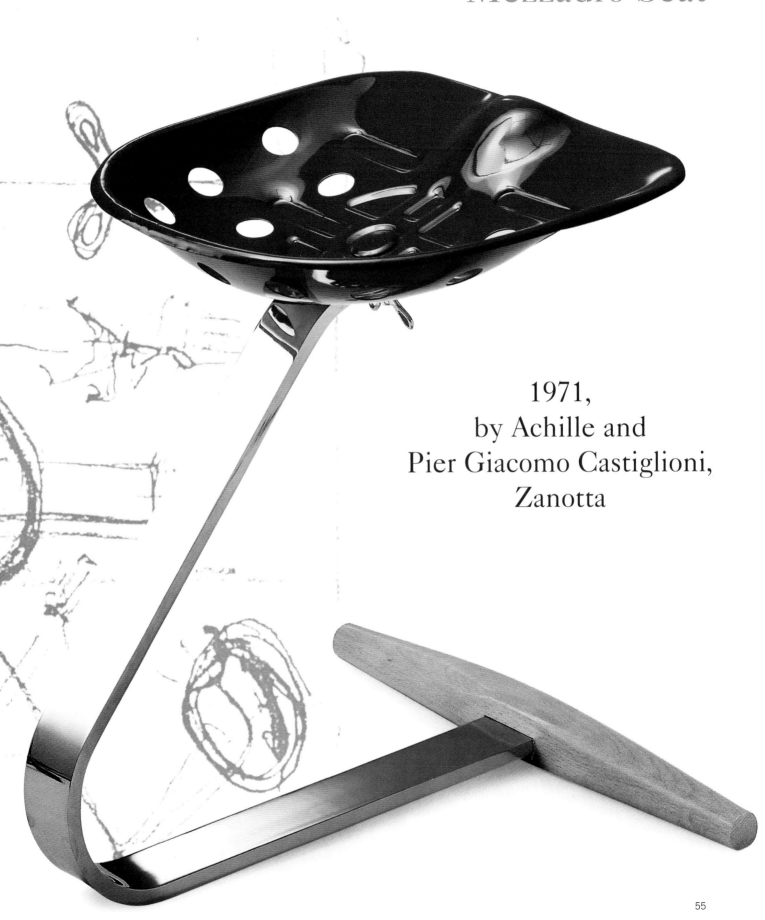

1971,
by Achille and
Pier Giacomo Castiglioni,
Zanotta

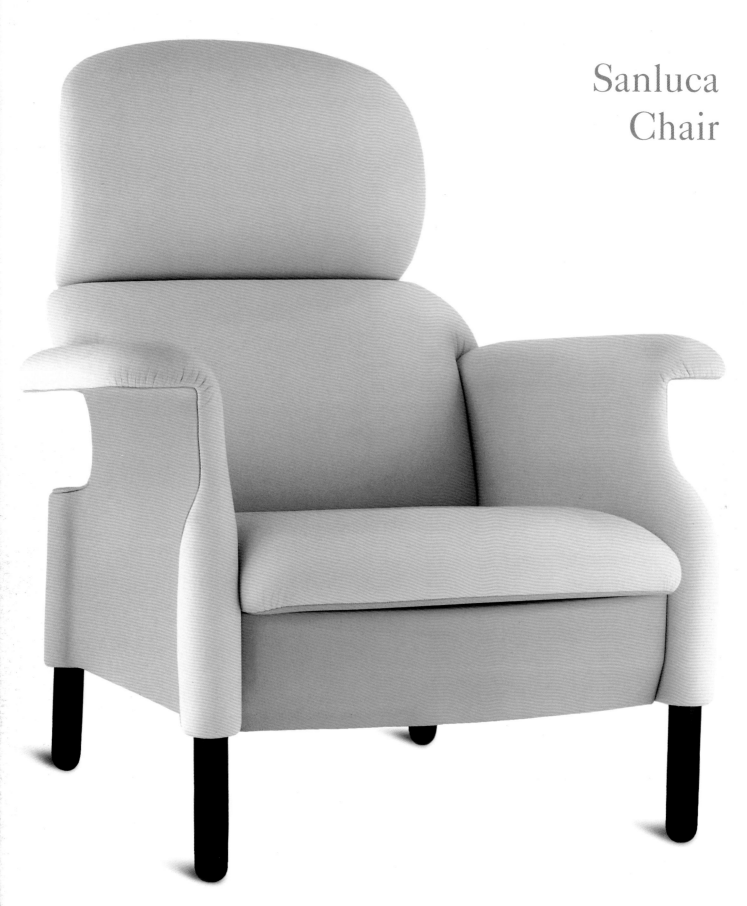

Sanluca Chair

1960, by Achille and Pier Giacomo Castiglioni,
now Poltrona Frau

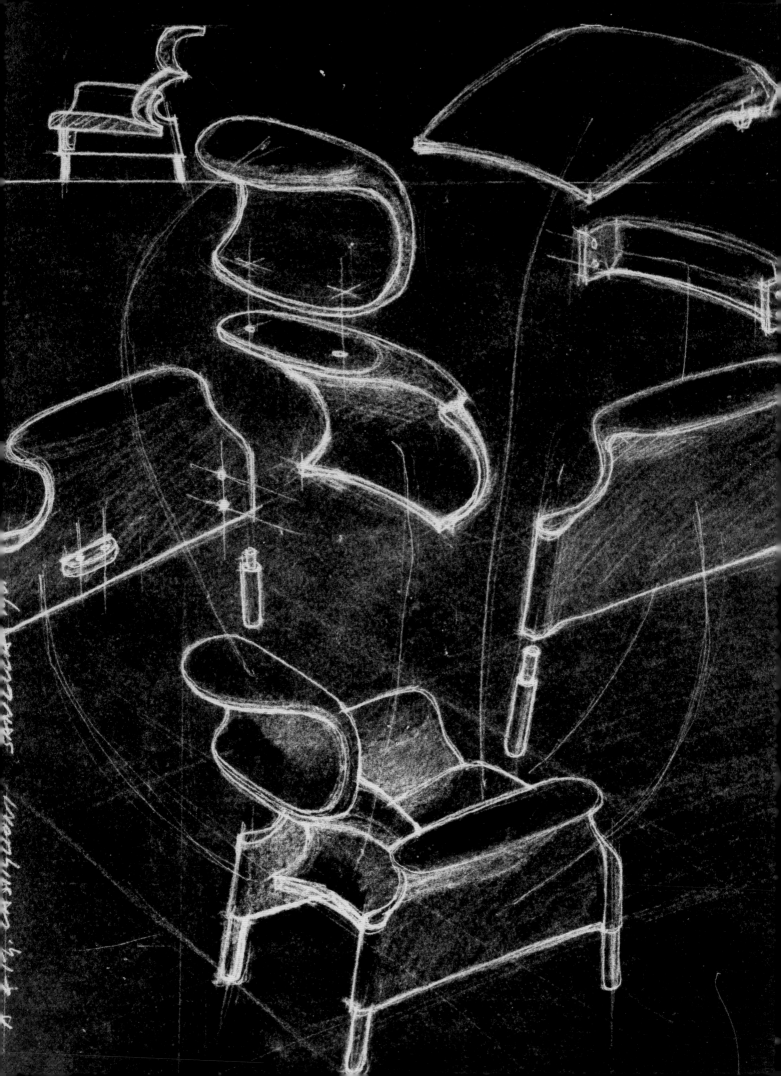

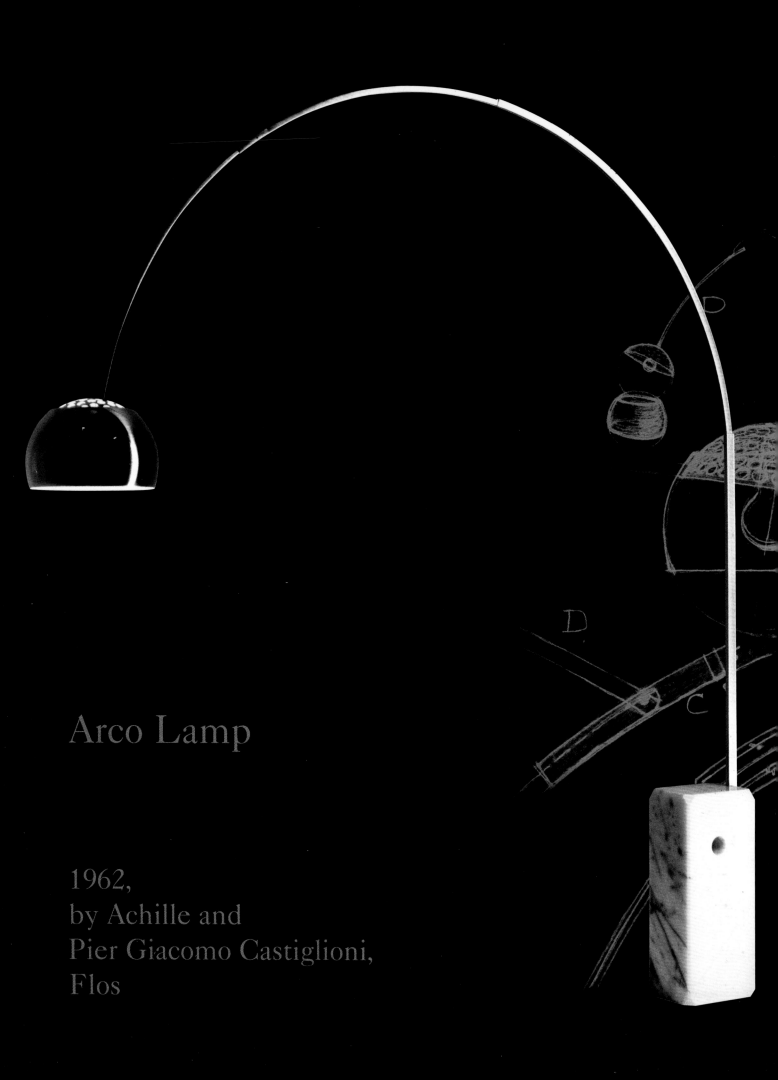

Arco Lamp

1962,
by Achille and
Pier Giacomo Castiglioni,
Flos

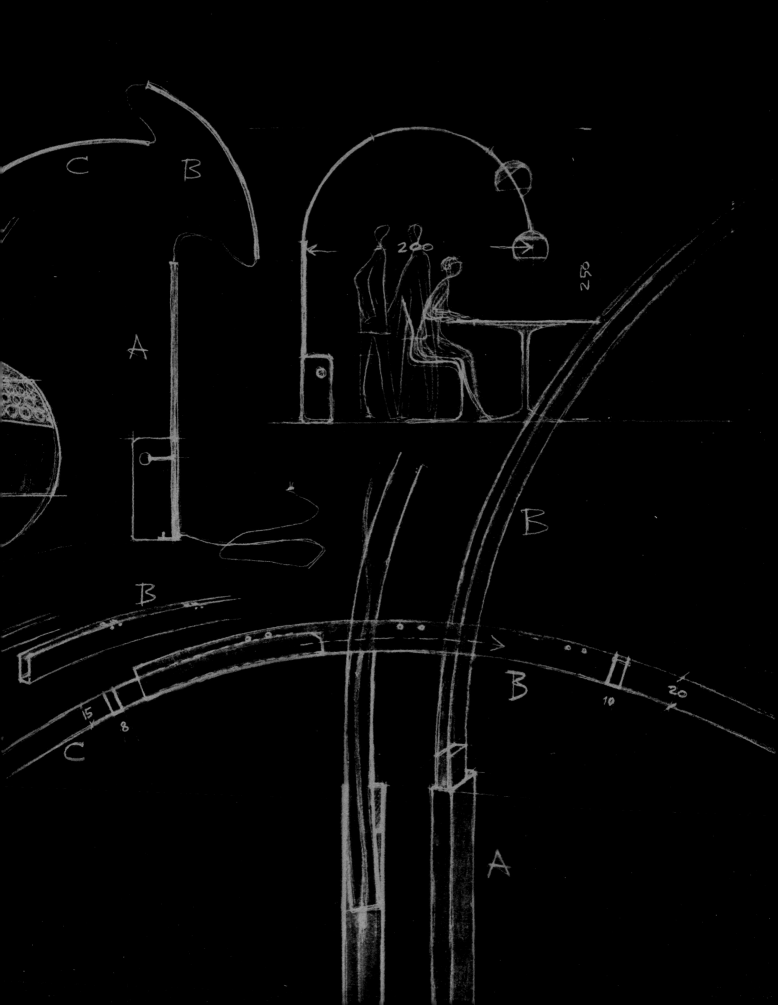

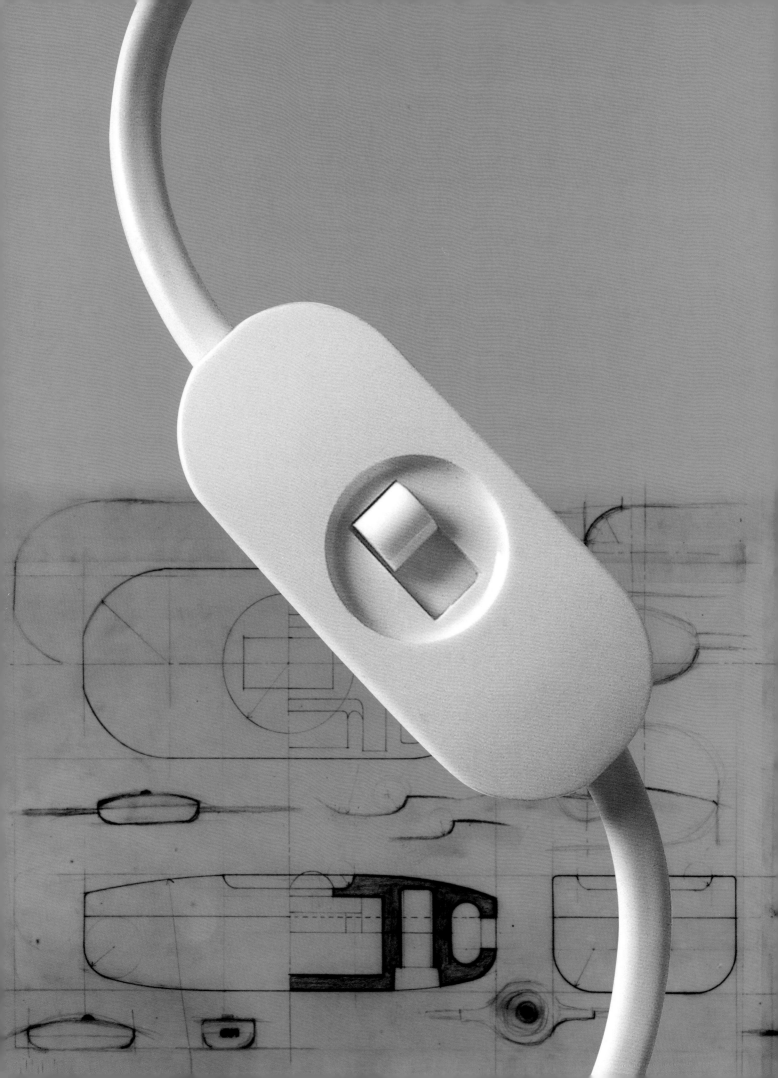

Rompitratta
On-Off Switch

1968, by Achille and Pier Giacomo Castiglioni, VLM

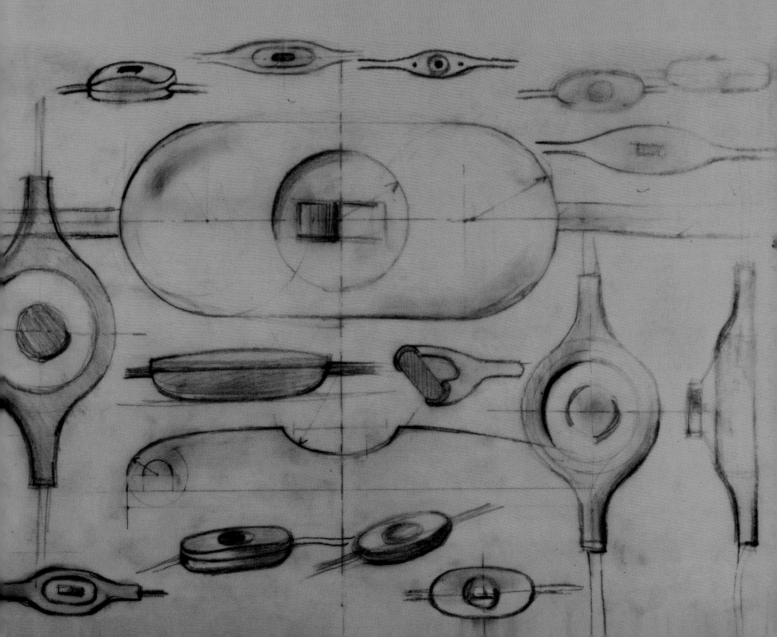

Joe Colombo

Architect (Milan, 1930-1971), studied at the Academy of Fine Arts in Brera and later at the Polytechnic in Milan. He opened a design studio and, in his brief career, obtained recognition and two Compasso d'Oro awards. His vision, which focused on the future, is evident in his later designs, the result of artistic, scientific, technological and methodological research: like the Total Furnishing Unit, the programmable T14 System for living (living machines which minimize living space) and multi-functional products.

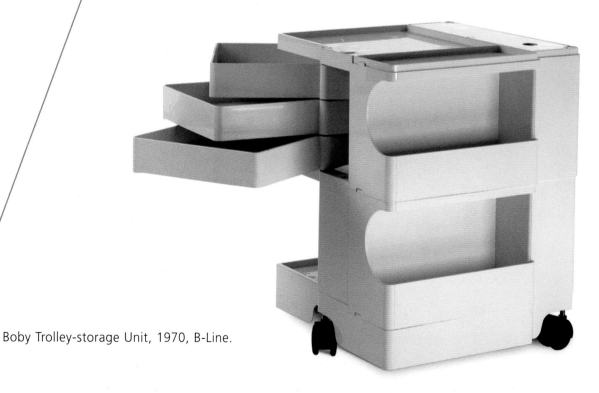

Boby Trolley-storage Unit, 1970, B-Line.

Elda Chair

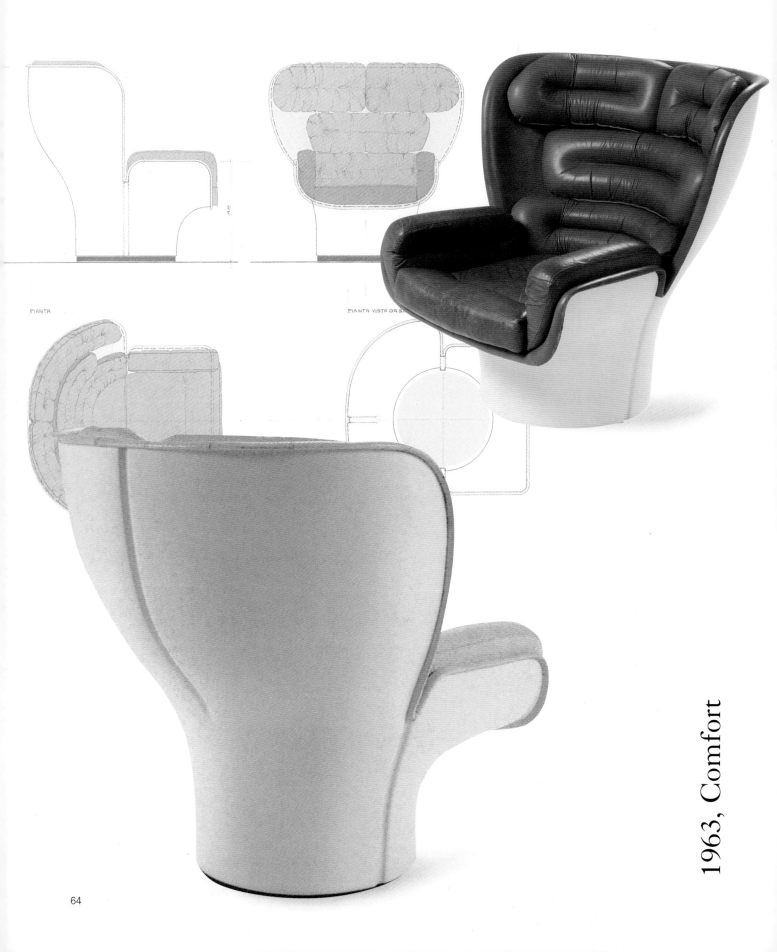

PIANTA

PIANTA VISTA DA S...

1963, Comfort

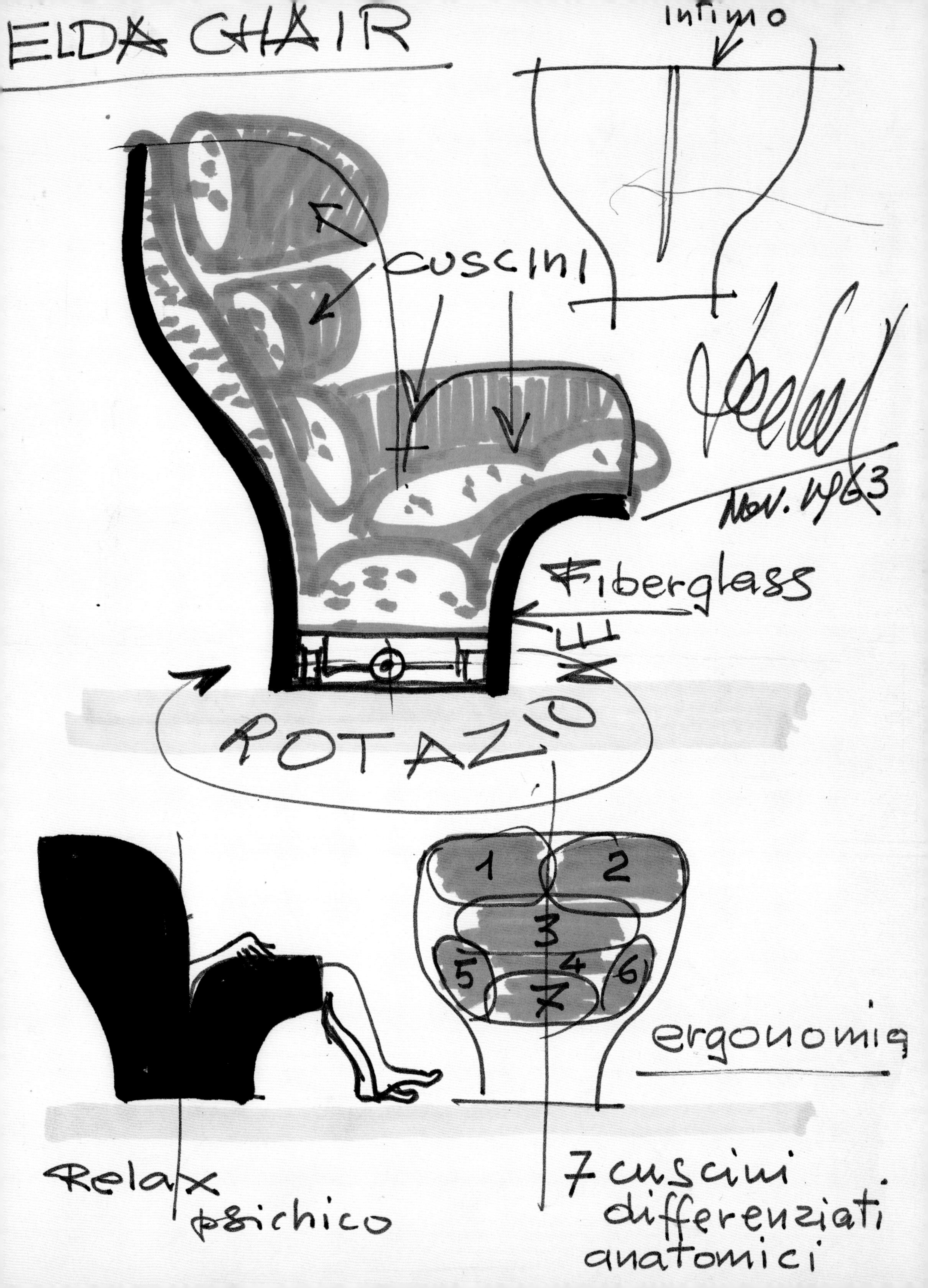

ELDA CHAIR

intimo

cuscini

Fiberglass

Nov. 1963

ROTAZIONE

1 2
3
5 4 6
7

ergonomia

Relax
psichico

7 cuscini
differenziati
anatomici

Kitchen Unit
Mini-Kitchen

1963, Boffi

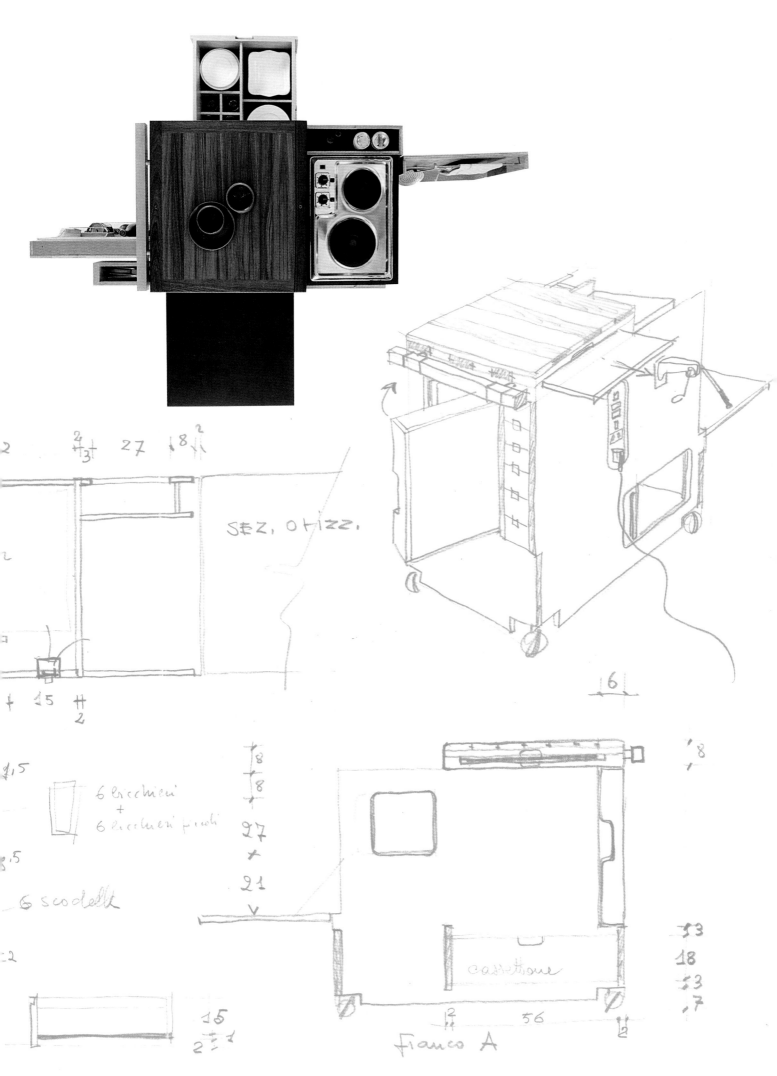

SEZ. OHIZZ.

6 bicchieri
+
6 bicchieri piccoli

6 scodelle

cassettone

Fianco A

Vico
Magistretti

Eclisse Table Lamp, 1967, Artemide.

Architect (Milan, 1920-2006), at the beginning of his career in the postwar reconstruction period he was dedicated primarily to architecture. At the same time, he became a recognized protagonist in the early stages of the design industry. In 1956 he was among the founder members of the ADI (Association for Industrial Design). He also lectured in Italy and abroad and he alternated his intense architectural activity with that of a prolific designer of furniture, furnishings, lamps and objects for which he received three Compasso d'Oro awards.

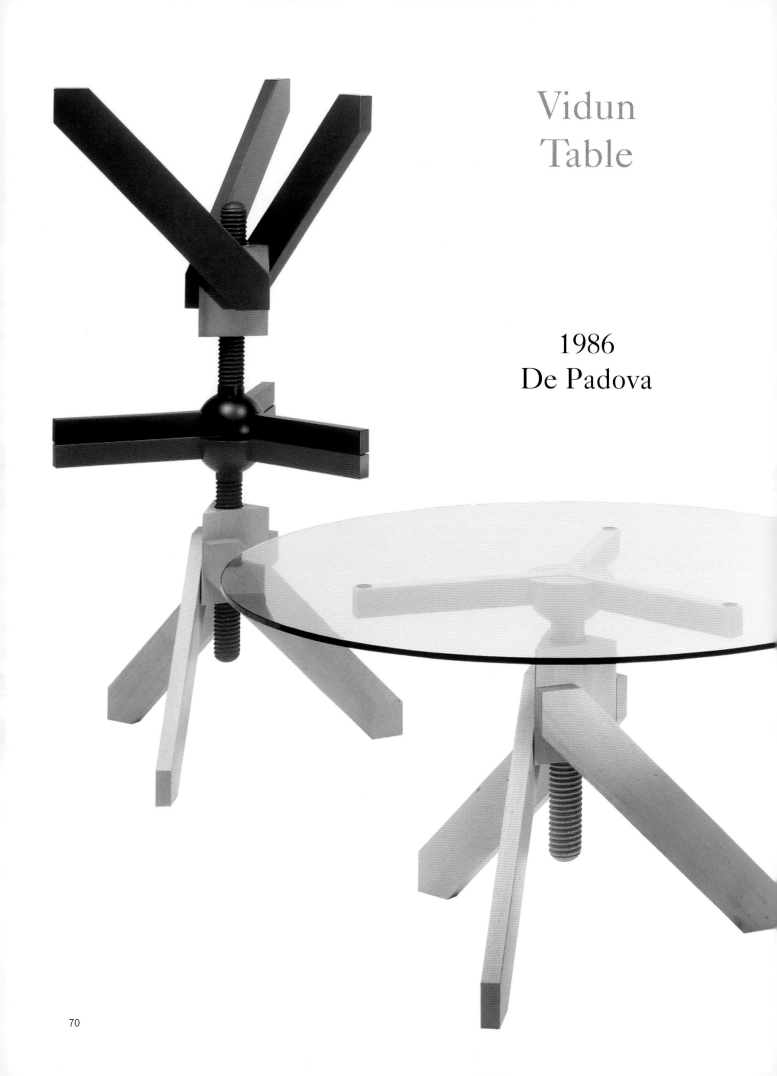

Vidun
Table

1986
De Padova

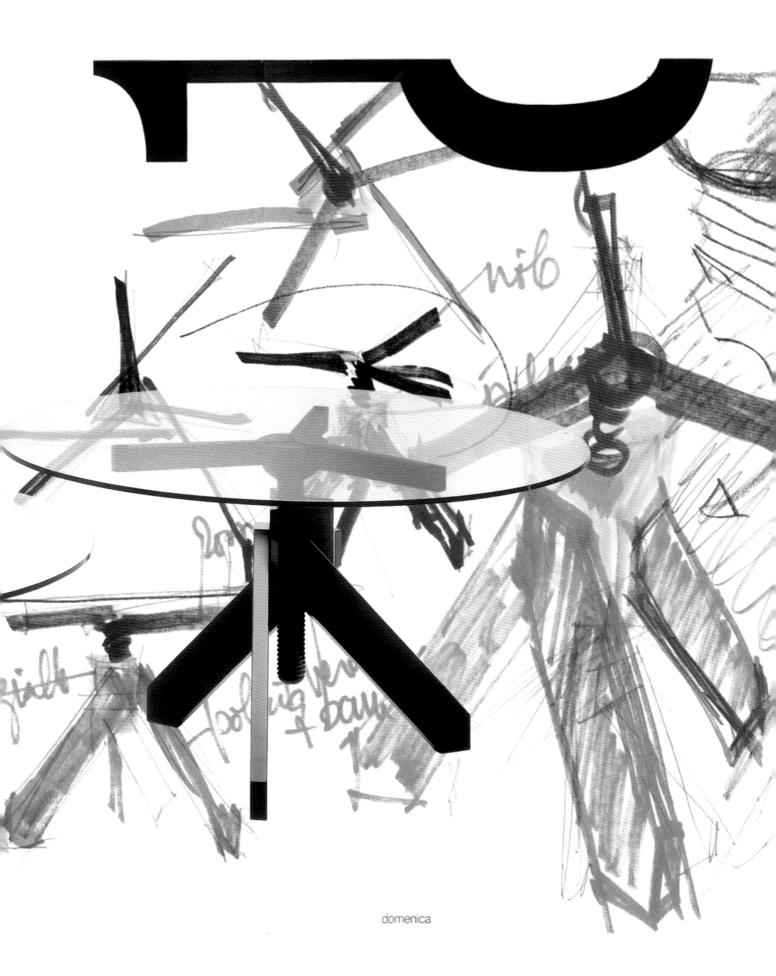

domenica

Atollo/Lamp

1977, Oluce

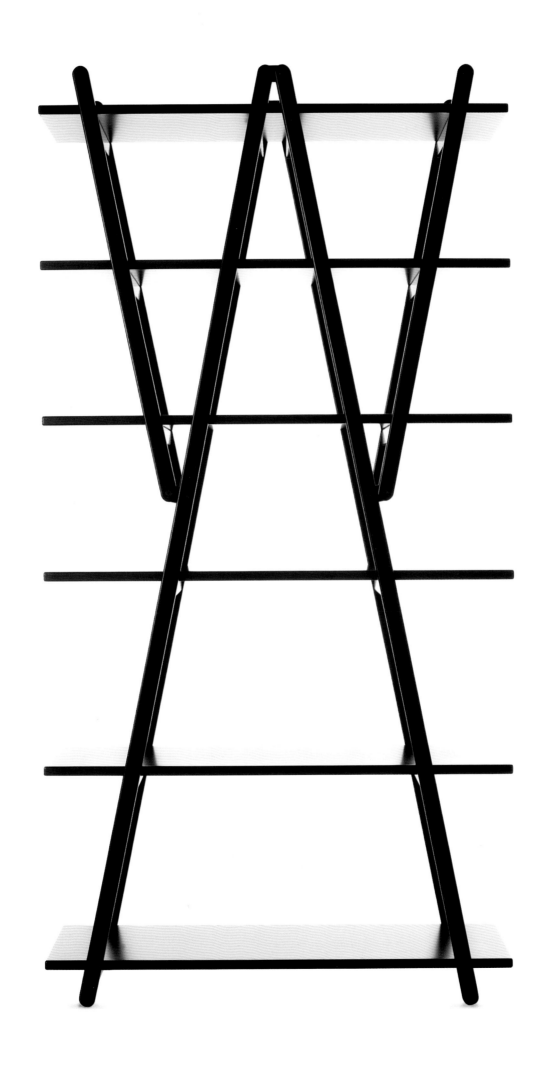

Nuvola Rossa Designer Wooden Shelf

1977, Cassina

Louisiana Chair

1993, De Padova

Bruno Munari

Artist (Milan, 1907-1998) and exponent in the first half of the 20th century of Arte Programmata (Programmed Art). He became the multifaceted protagonist experimenting with different disciplines, which are difficult to classify in the fields which he went in and out of with legendary nonchalance: from editorial design to painting, from sculpture to poetry and on to teaching, mostly in relation to games and childhood. He received three Compasso d'Oro awards, as well as significant international recognition. He left a rich legacy of visual works of art and a vast editorial production, as well as several designs for the furniture industry and that of *objets d'art*.

Cubo Ashtray, 1957, Danese.

1945, now Zanotta

Zizi the Monkey
Toy

1952, Pigomma Singer,
now new CLAC edition

Book:
"Le forchette di Munari"
(Munari's Forks)

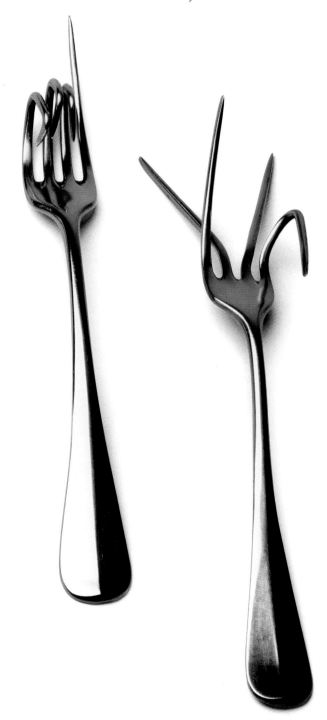

1959, Muggiani
2008, reprinted by Corraini

1964, Danese

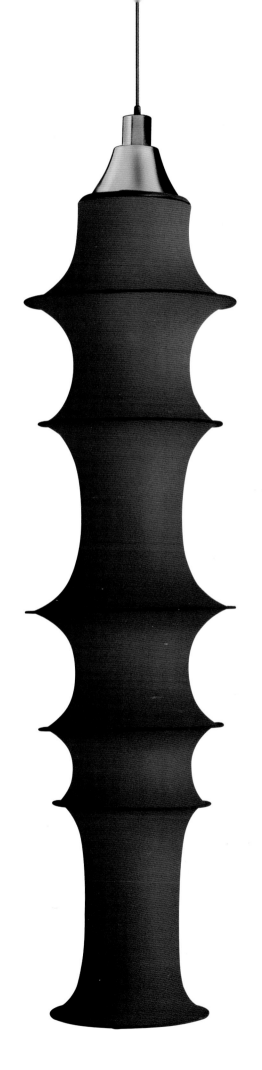

1971, Robots

Ettore
Sottsass

Architect (Innsbruck, 1917-Milan, 2007) with many interests, worked for thirty years with Olivetti. He received seven Compasso d'Oro awards (one for the design of a computer in 1959). He participated in the Alchimia group and then founded Memphis in 1981.

He was a protagonist in the renewal of design. His shapes are archetypal forms in primary colors, which he assembles and takes to pieces with irony like playing with building bricks, giving rise to symbolic-monumental pieces which tend to be exciting before being functional.

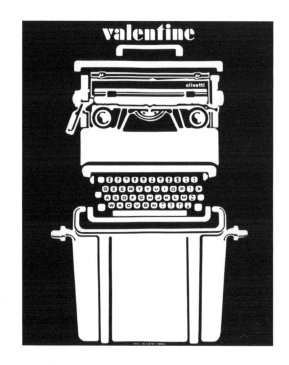

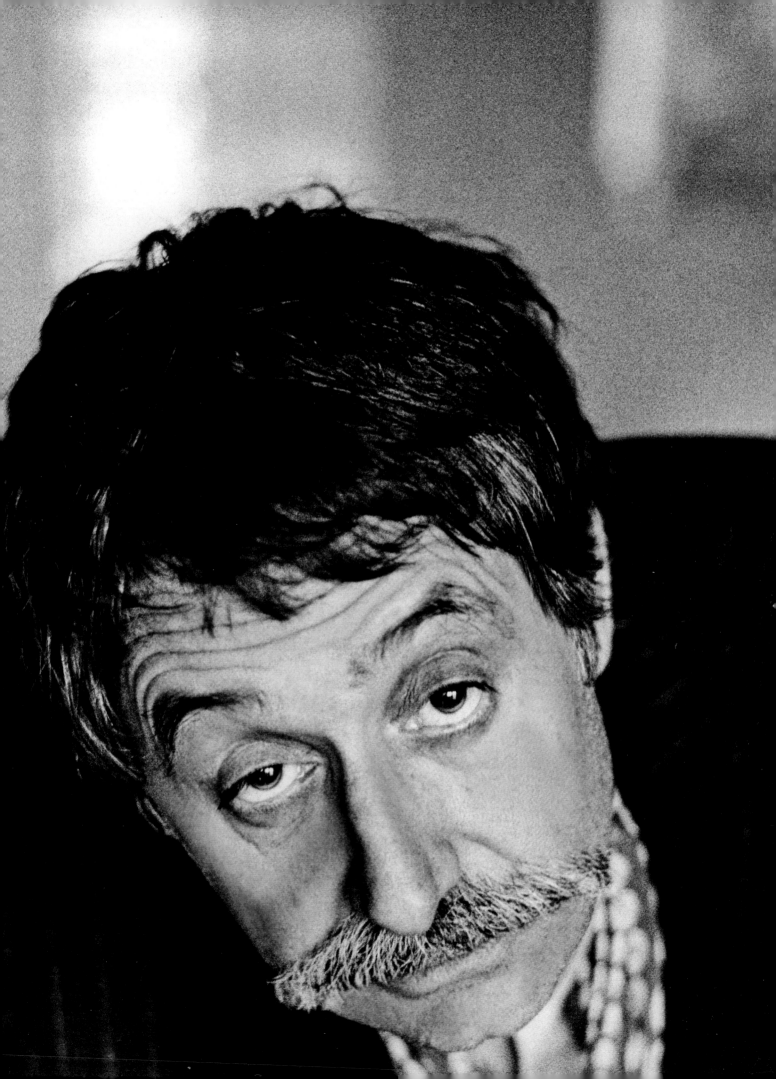

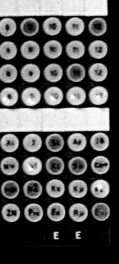

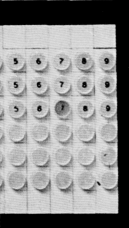

Electronic Calculator / Elea 9003

1959, Olivetti

Valentine
Typewriter

1969, Olivetti

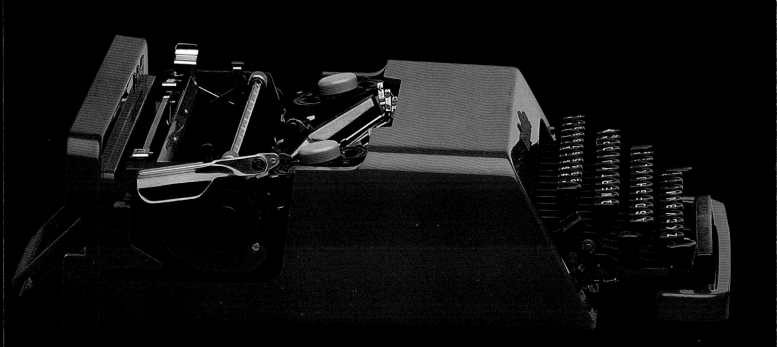

Marco Zanuso

Town planning architect (Milan, 1916-2001), in the period immediately after the war contributed to the debate on the Movimento Moderno (Modern Movement). He was considered the founding father of design and one of the first to study the industrialization of products and to experiment with new technology and materials, like, for example, foam rubber. He worked as editor in the magazines Domus (1947-49), Casabella (1952-54) and taught for thirty years at the Polytechnic in Milan. He received seven Compasso d'Oro awards.

Algol Television, 1964, by Marco Zanuso and Richard Sapper, Brionvega.

Lady
Chair

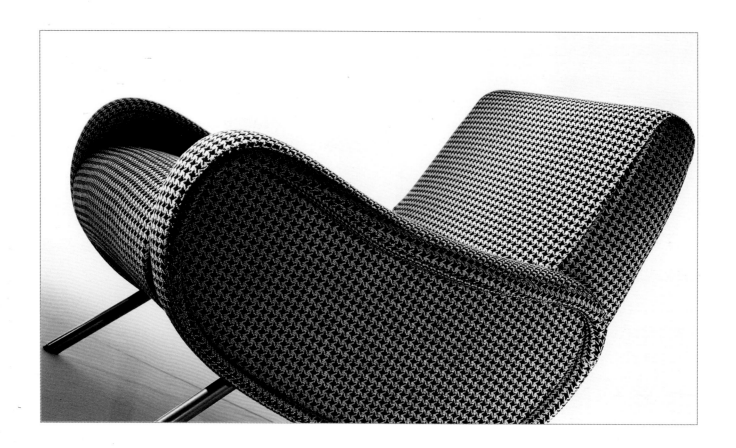

1951
Arflex

ts502
Radio alarm clock

1963, by Marco Zanuso and Richard Sapper, Brionvega

Children's Chair
Model 1999

1964, by Marco Zanuso
and Richard Sapper, Kartell

the present under attack

Winds of change blowing from the United States to Europe from the mid Sixties and Seventies and later, shook architecture and industrial design to their very foundations, even in Italy. It was called radical and it was explicit, even in its definition, in the idea of questioning the roots of the discipline, including even the arts. To cries of "All culture is repressive," the protest movement, headed by individuals or by durable design groups, issued proposals and theoretical manifestos with political overtones, sympathizing with the socio-economic malaise which permeated the country. Architecture, having refuted the precepts of Rationalism and the Movimento Moderno, moved toward a spontaneous and popular form of creativity which was less conditioned by cultural formats and hypothesized a reformulation of methods and ideologies. Design was inspired by the basic crafts, by a national mass form of kitsch and no less by Pop Art. In Florence, where there was mass participation in student demonstrations, "Anti" groups proliferated, exploring new models of urban structures and in a series of experimental seminars and workshops reaffirming utopias and the desire the de-stabilize design and the institutional profession. Stepping in the footsteps of Florence, Milan followed suit, with the city's Polytechnic in particular becoming a protagonist of provocative cultural and design impulses.

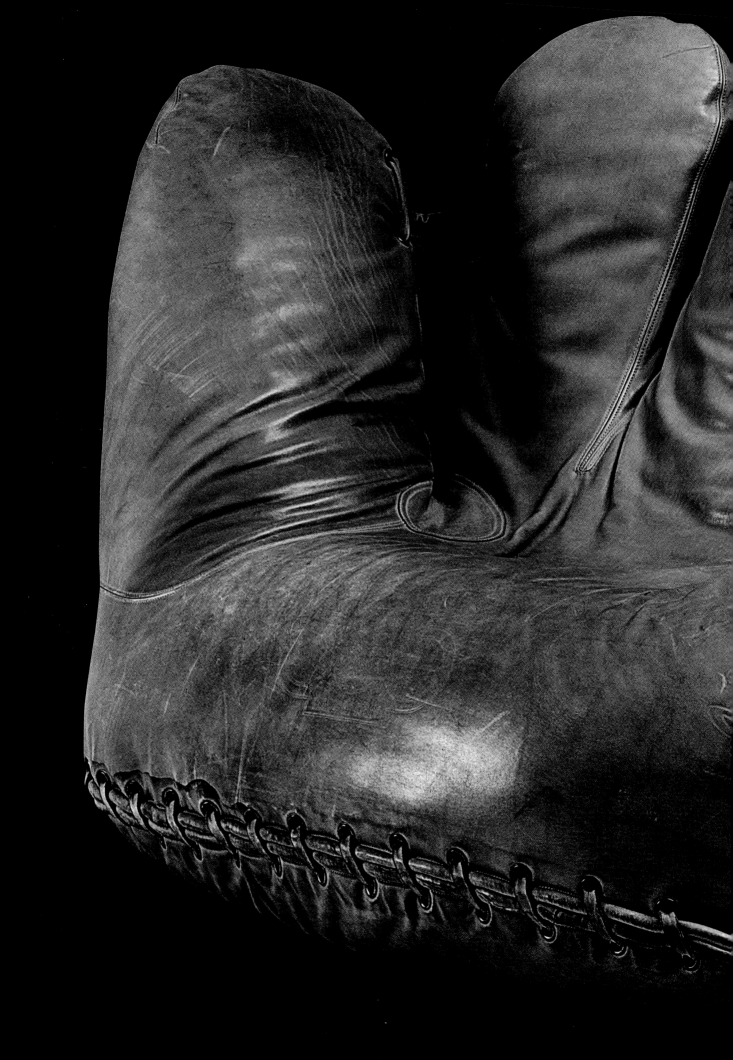

Alchimia

reated by Alessandro and Adriana Guerriero in Milan in 1976, it united designers associated by the experience of the radical design of the Seventies. This workshop produced exhibitions, publications and "theoretical manifestos" and explored all the fields of design. Under the directorship of Alessandro Mendini, it gave rise to furniture, objects, fashion, graphics and decoration, both in artisan form as well as on an industrial scale by designers such as Ettore Sottsass, Paola Navone, Michele De Lucchi, Andrea Branzi (the last ones met in the Memphis group in 1981) and by many young designers. It received a Compasso d'Oro award in 1981.

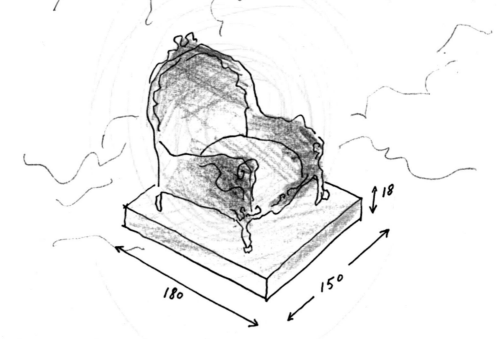

Proust Chair

1978
Alessandro Mendini

Sinerpica Lamp

LAMPADA
"SINERPICA ANGOLOSA"
REALIZZATA IN METALLO
GENN. 1978
h · 60 CM
NON PRODOTTA

1979, Michele De Lucchi

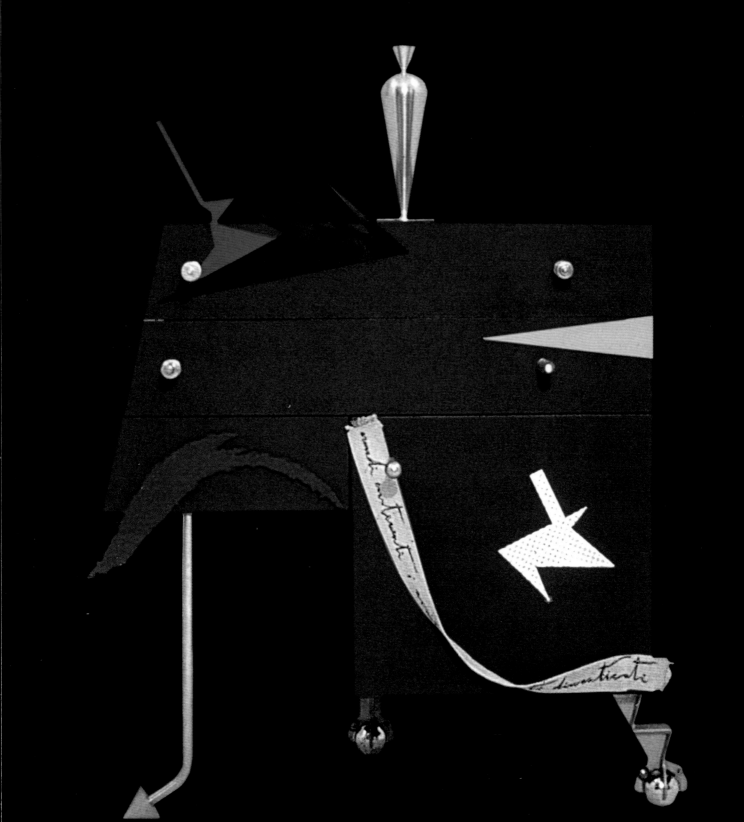

1981, Alessandro Mendini with various designers

Archizoom
Associates

Founded in Florence (1966-1974) by Andrea Branzi, Gilberto Corretti, Paolo Deganello, Massimo Morozzi, Dario and Lucia Bartolini. It began in the period of protest with its activity aimed at architecture and urban research, formulating some themes of the radical movement, a trend which also took root in other countries. Subsequently, it concentrated on the renewal of design through exhibitions and installations, furnishing accessories and dressing design projects as well as essays and theoretical articles in the major international magazines.

Mies Chair,
1969, Poltronova.

Superonda
(Easy Chair elements)

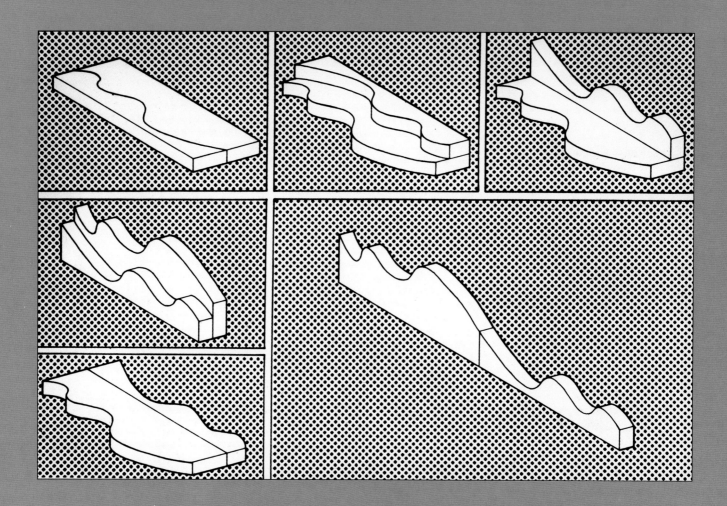

1966

Poltronova

Safari Sofa

1967, Poltronova

Memphis

Founded in 1981 by Ettore Sottsass and by young architects who trained in his firm (including Aldo Cibic, Michele De Lucchi, Matteo Thun), as well as many other designers, both Italian and foreign, attracted by a lively cultural climate and by an incisive iconography. It produced objects, fabrics, silver objects, lamps and laminates of which the surfaces became the unmistakable symbol of the designs. The theorist of the group is Barbara Radice; she is also its art director.

Super / Lamp

1981
Martine Bedin

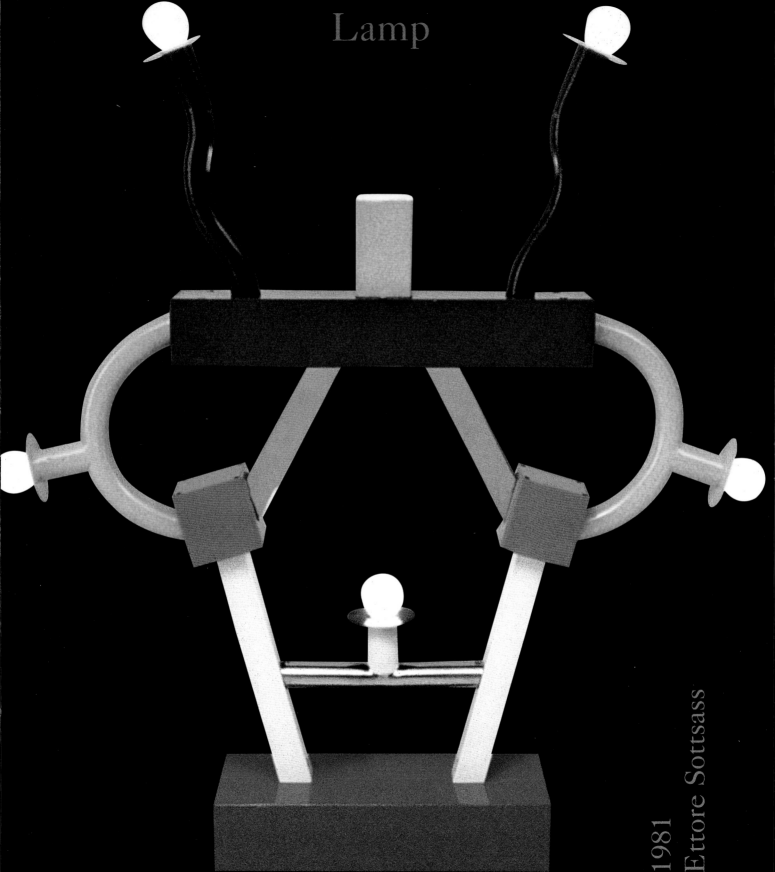

Carlton / Bookcase

Kristall / Table

1981, Michele De Lucchi

lone wolves

Some designers are difficult to classify in terms of conceptually or temporally defined stylistic currents. These were strong characters with a solid cultural and professional base, who had lived through decades of varying tendencies, distinguishing themselves in different fields, always in very original and personal ways.

And today they are in charge of large firms which welcome young people, many of whom are foreigners.

Emblematic figures, often recognizable due to their eclectic and incisive designs, capable of leaving a mark in the history of Italian design: some in the pursuit of rigor, method and functionalism in a coherent and refined way, others following a strong vocation in non-fiction and in publishing, others more inclined to ethico-ecological design and others still who have a strong tendency toward team design capable of appreciating young talents.

Mario
Bellini

Architect (Milan, 1935), a teacher and manager of the magazine *Domus* (1986-1991), has dedicated himself to industrial design and furnishings winning the Compasso d'Oro award four times. He is currently involved mainly in architecture. With a complex personality, always hovering between architecture and industrial design, he says that he is against design without culture.

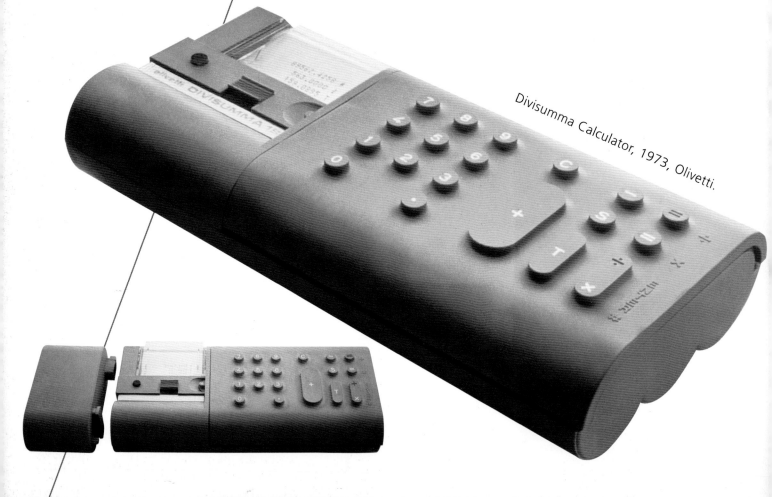

Divisumma Calculator, 1973, Olivetti.

Cab 412 / Chair

1977, Cassina

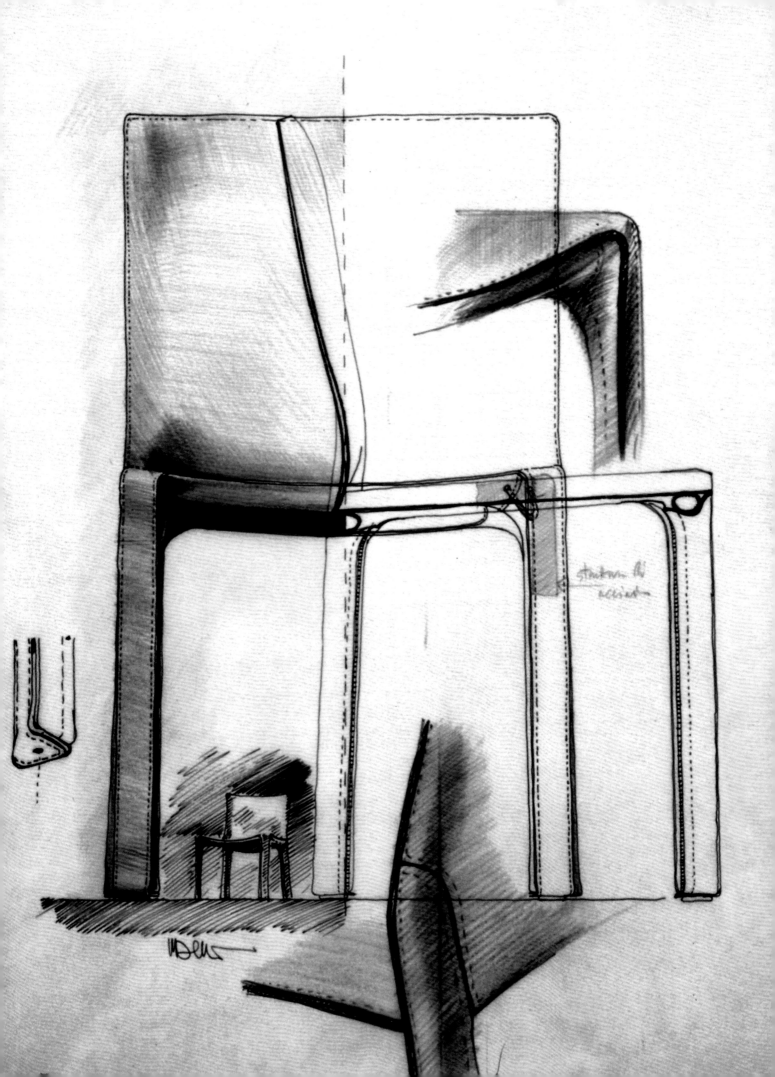

struttura in
acciaio

1972, B&B Italia

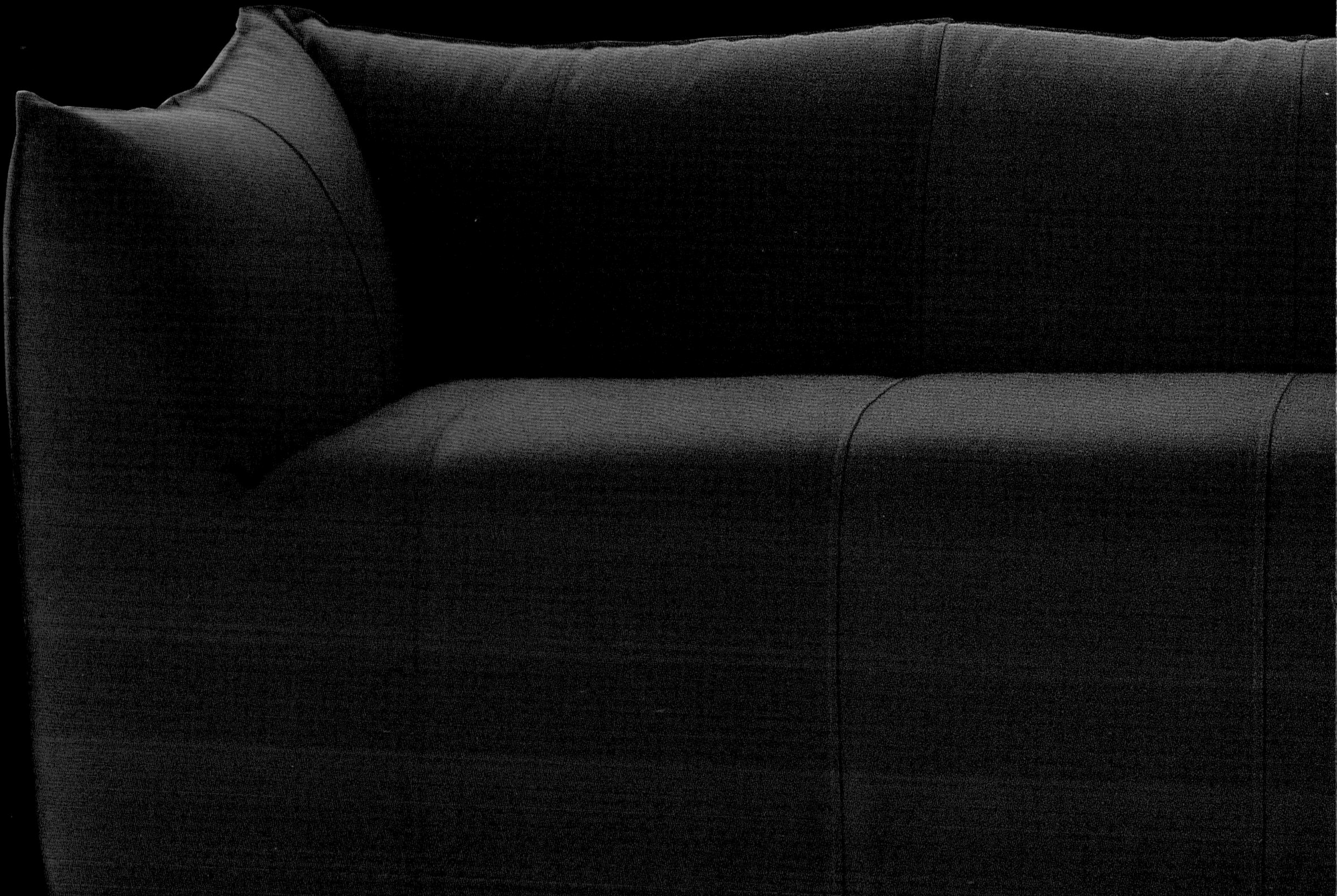

Cini
Boeri

Architect (Milan, 1924), founded his own studio in 1963 in Milan and worked on architectural design above all for homes and interior design. He experimented with pioneering and avant-garde materials such as rubber, polyurethane and plastic for the classical furnishing products. The rigor of design is its own distinguishing mark, architectural training prevails over the role of designer. He confirms that his furnishings were always conceived for his own interiors and, only subsequently, mass produced.

Tre B Handle, 1982, Fusital.

Serpentone Sofa

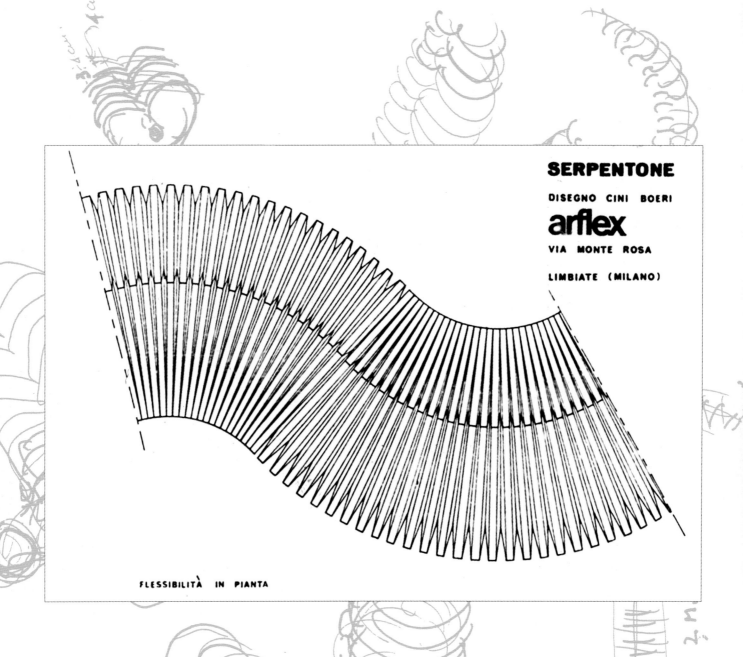

SERPENTONE

DISEGNO CINI BOERI

arflex

VIA MONTE ROSA

LIMBIATE (MILANO)

FLESSIBILITÀ IN PIANTA

1971, Arflex

Strips
Sofa

1972, Arflex

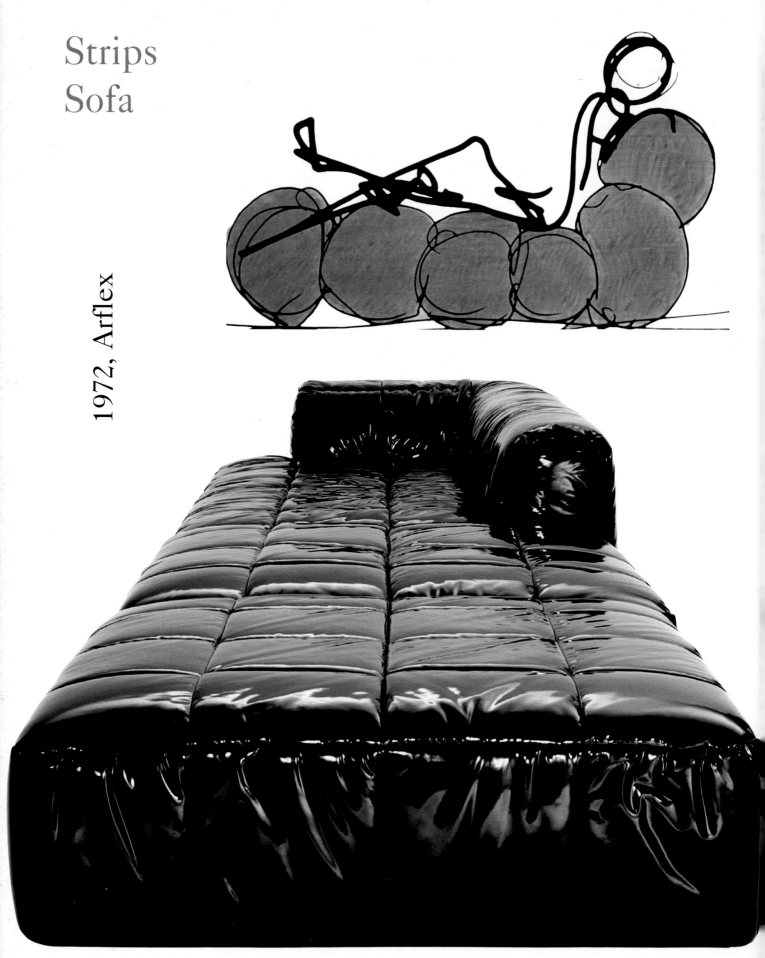

Ghost / Chair

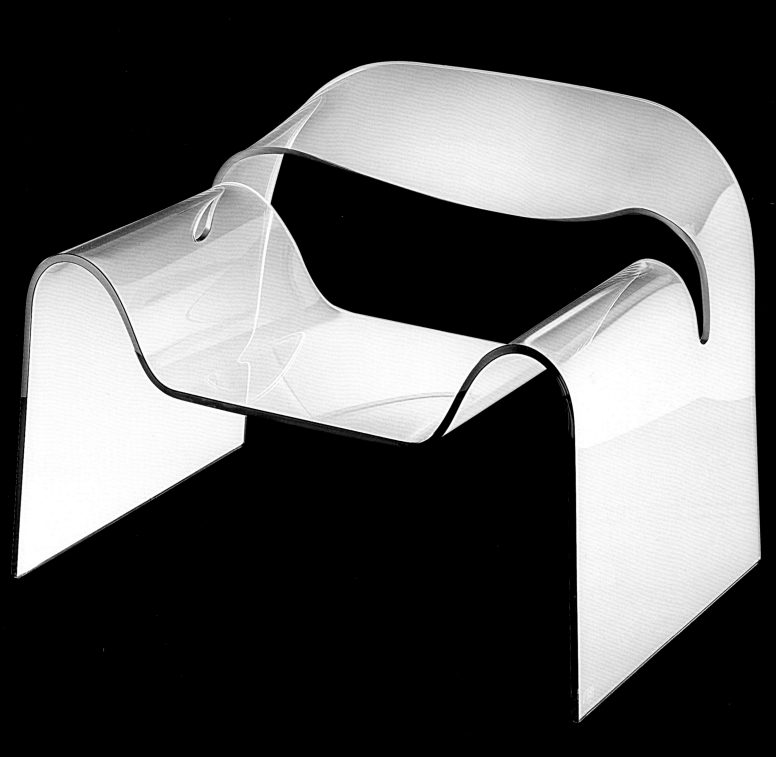

1987, Fiam Italia

Andrea Branzi

Architect (Florence, 1938), one of the founders of Archizoom Associates (1964-1974); exponent of the radical movement he was involved in industrial and experimental design, architecture and town planning. His work was dominated by a theoretical objective on the changes in the culture of design in relation to the socio-technological context. He has written essays and books on the theory of design and on the history of Italian design. From 1984 to 1987 he directed the magazine Modo. He was among the founders of the Domus Academy and was, for a time, its educational director. He designs furniture and poetic and anthropomorphic objects.

Toothpick Holder, 1991, Alessi.

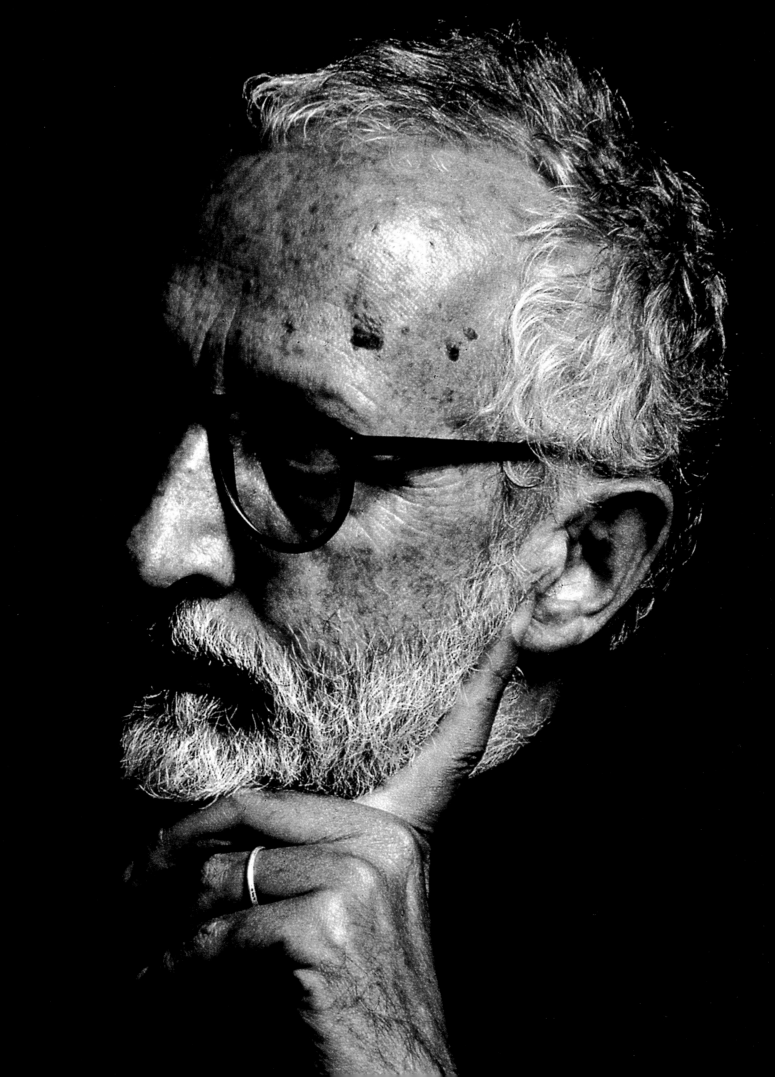

Domestic Animals
Furniture Collection

1985
Zabro-Zanotta

Project
Genetic Tales

2000, Alessi

Enzo
Mari

Artist (Novara, 1932), has extensive experience in Arte Programmata (Programmed Art). He was later involved in graphics and in the design of objects and won the Compasso d'Oro Award three times. Known as the "critical conscience" of design he is the author of controversial essays, pamphlets on the role of the profession and on loyalty to a basic principle: improving the quality of objects while keeping an eye on production costs.

Tonietta Chair, 1985, Zanotta.

16 animals
Construction Toy

1957, Danese

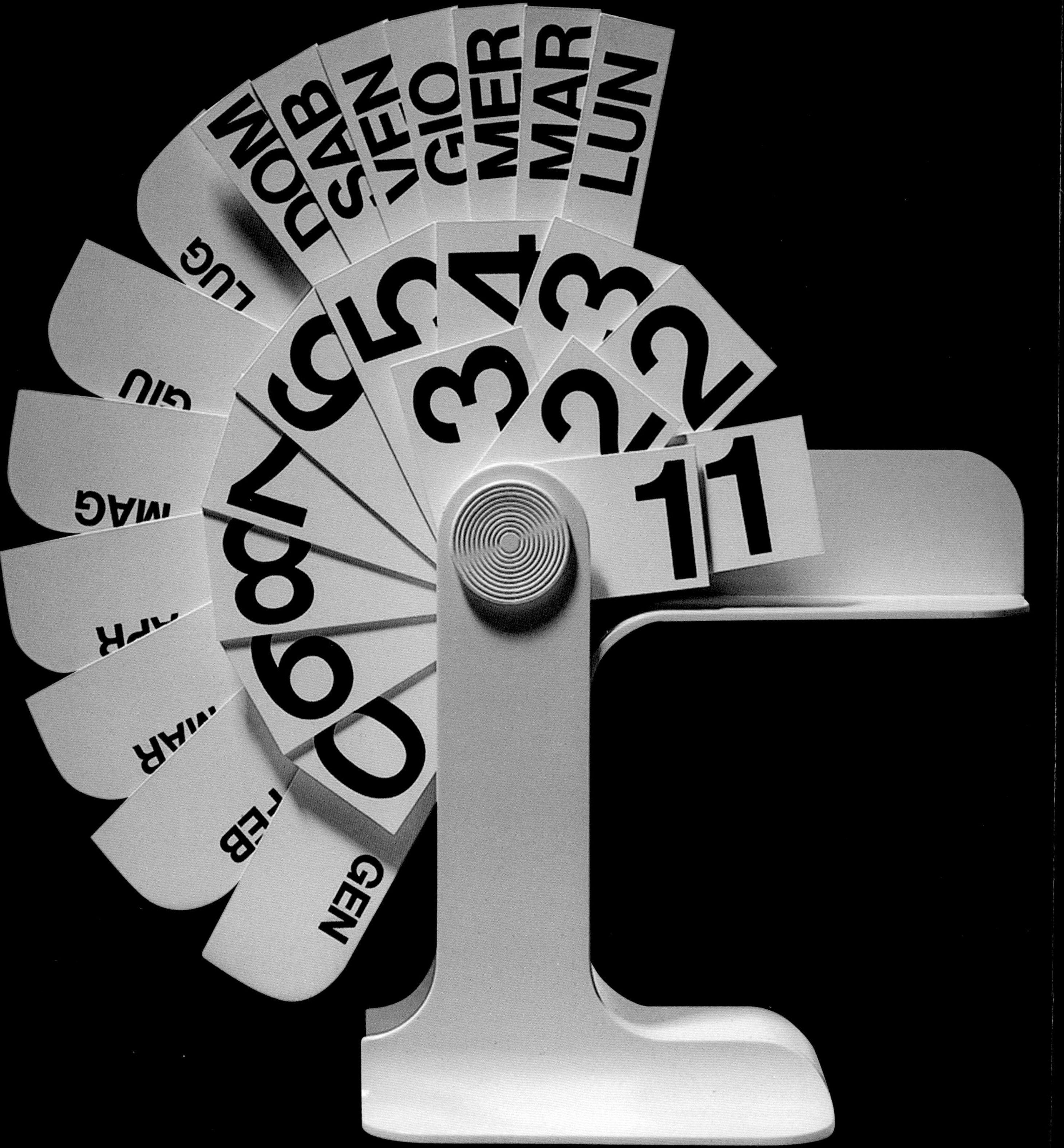

LUN
MAR
MER
GIO
VEN
SAB
DOM
LUG
GIU
MAG
APR
MAR
FEB
GEN
11

Timor
Perpetual Calendar

1967, Danese

1976, Artemide

Alessandro Mendini

Architect (Milan, 1931), managed the magazine *Casabella* (1970-1976), *Modo* (1977-1983), *Domus* (1979-1986), where he expressed and theorized avant-garde culture, from radical design to post-modern, from kitsch to banal with a view of the transversality of styles and the intertwining of the arts. An eclectic designer with a personal aesthetic vocabulary, he also produced architectural works with his brother, Francesco. With a provocative and controversial method of design that he defines as sentimental, he focused attention on marginal and non-institutional cultures and applied the artist's temperament to architecture and design.

Anna G. Corkscrew, 1994, Alessi.

Lots of dots
Watch

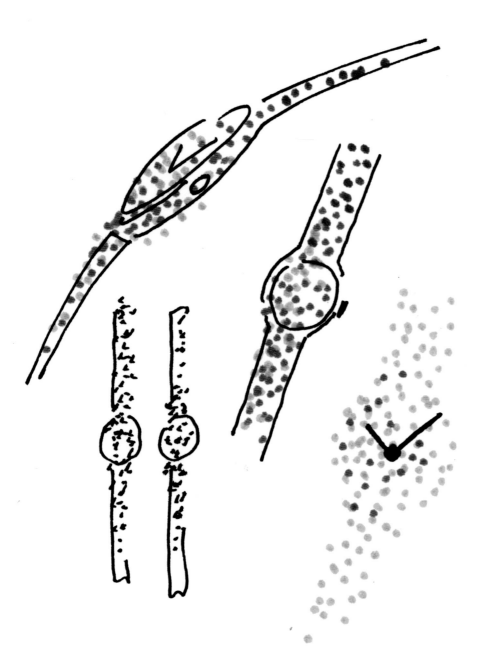

1992, Swatch

IMPRESSIONISTA

INTER
CONTINENTALE

IL GRANDE
E IL PIÙ
PICCOLO

UGUALI

TIPO
OROLOGIO
PORCELLANA
DEL
SETTECENTO

SUL POP
APPROCCIO
AUTONOMO
RISPETTO
A SWATCH

Alessandro M. Corkscrew

2003, Alessi

COLLEZIONI NUMERATE A TERMINE ? — PREVEDERE DEI TREND

CONCETTO SWATCH — 100%

arlecchino clown sfumatura india SVIZZERO

malevic africa new age indiani d'america

delft SPAZIALE SOMELLIER

COLLEZIONE DI SOLDATINI

today and tomorrow

Reports on contemporary Italian industrial design paint a particularly varied panorama, albeit distinguished by some common denominators: established names with large firms like design "machines," increasingly closer relationships between designers and production companies, and the worldwide exportation of pure Italian taste in reading tendencies and interpreting the reality of objects. Today's protagonists and those of tomorrow, young exponents often brought into the limelight by a small successful design, maneuver between new technology and innovative materials, not disdaining occasional forays into unorthodox spheres, for example in self-production. Or into the realms of art and cartoons that are only apparently distant. Almost all self-referential, from the point of view of stylistic choices – the great masters have not left disciples but only a sort of respect for the profession and a certain design ethic – Italian designers can consider themselves a cultural resource of the country. Many of them are lecturers in the new faculties of industrial design and in the courses run by innumerable private design schools. Even though recently they must be on their guard and beware of their numerous and competitive foreign colleagues, who are also much appreciated by the public and above all by companies.

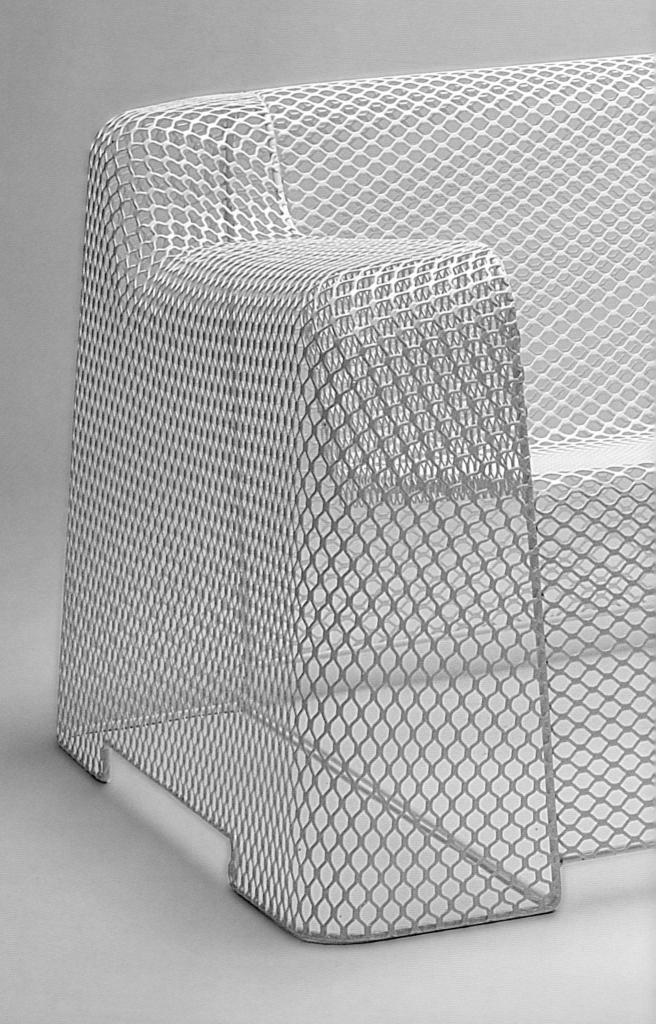

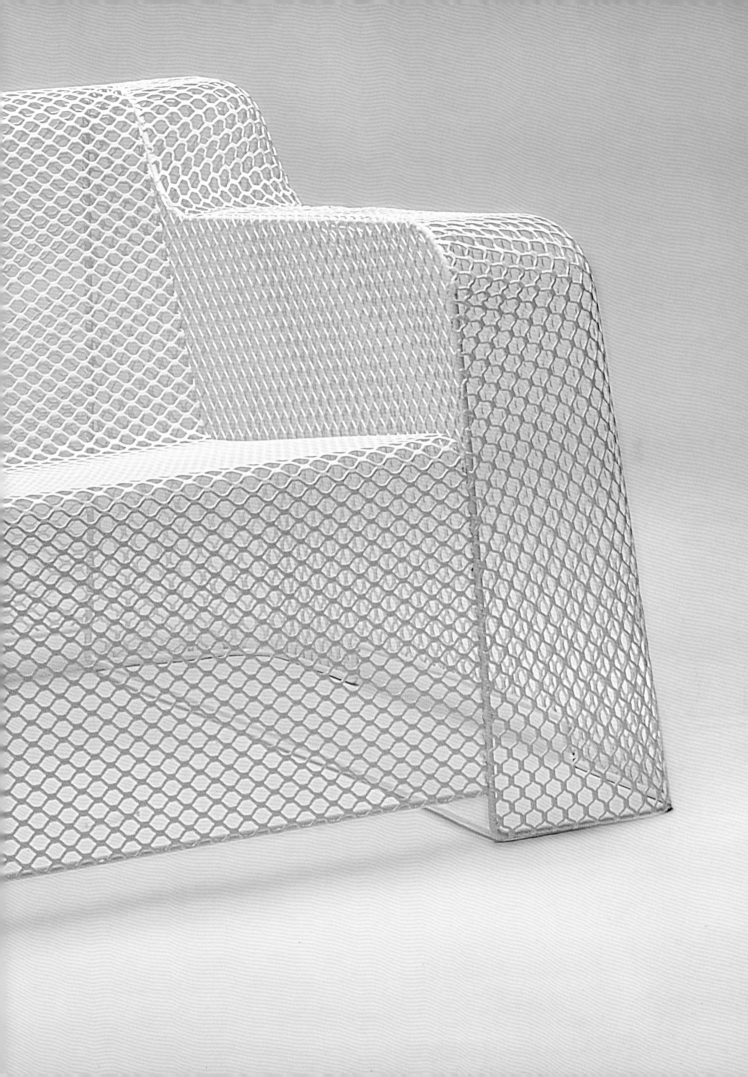

Antonio Citterio

Architect (Meda, 1950). Fully occupied with activities in both architecture and industrial design, working with numerous Italian and foreign companies. For a decade, until 1981, he worked with Paolo Nava. From 1987 to 1996 he was a partner of Terry Dwan and in 1999 he founded the firm, Antonio Citterio and Partners with Patricia Viel in Milan. Minimalist design, the definition of a plain, sober, linear style as was prevalent in the Nineties, was associated with his name. It was expressed with coherence and formal elegance in furniture, lamps, objects and interior design.

Lastra Lamp, 1998, Flos.

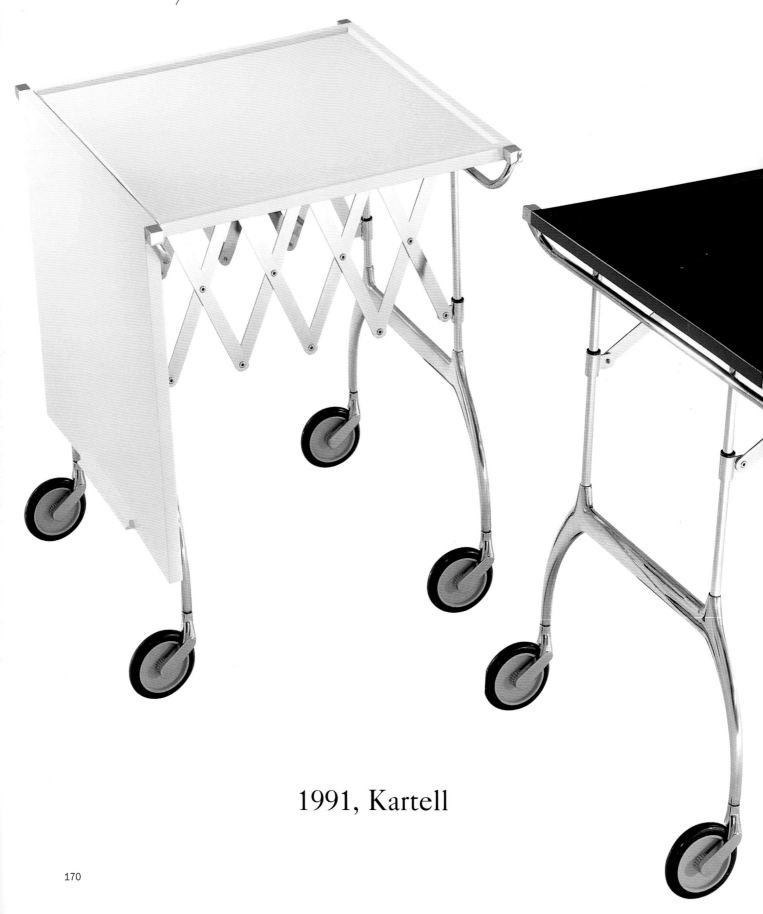

1991, Kartell

George / Sofa

2001, B&B Italia

Charles Sofa
1997, B&B Italia

Michele De Lucchi

Architect (Ferrara, 1951), founded the Cavart group in his university days in Florence, participated in cultural debates on radical design and designed pieces first for Alchimia and subsequently for Memphis. He continued his work in Milan in the Sotsass studio and he worked for Olivetti Synthesis until 1978. He opened his own firm in 1984 and produced architectural works and museum display settings, corporate image projects for private and public customers, he designed lamps, objects and furniture of a semi-artisan type even for his own brand, Produzione Privata.

Perseo Lamp, 2007, Produzione Privata.

Tolomeo Lamp

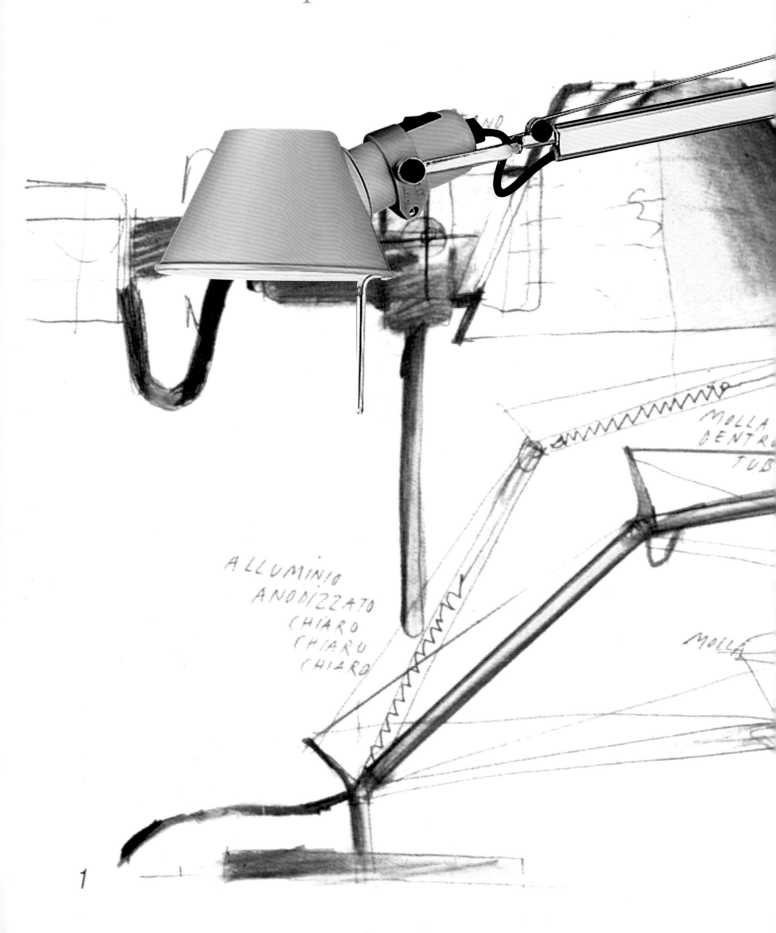

1

1987, Artemide

1987, Produzione Privata

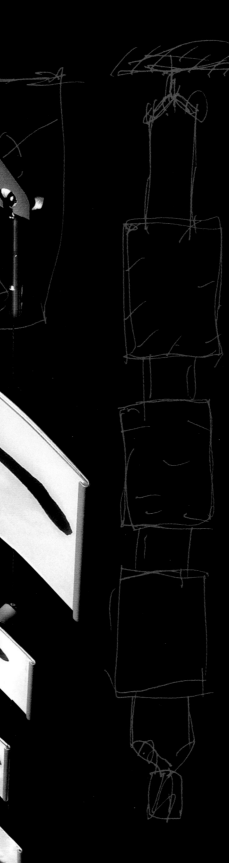

2002

Caimi Brevetti

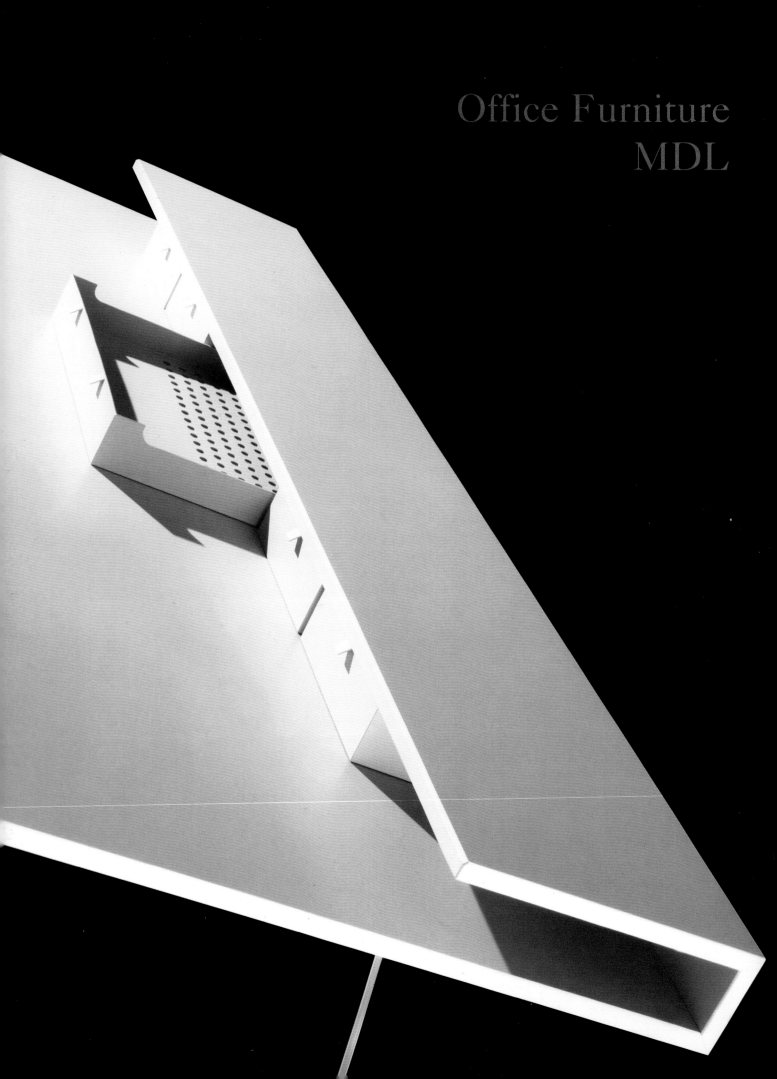

Office Furniture
MDL

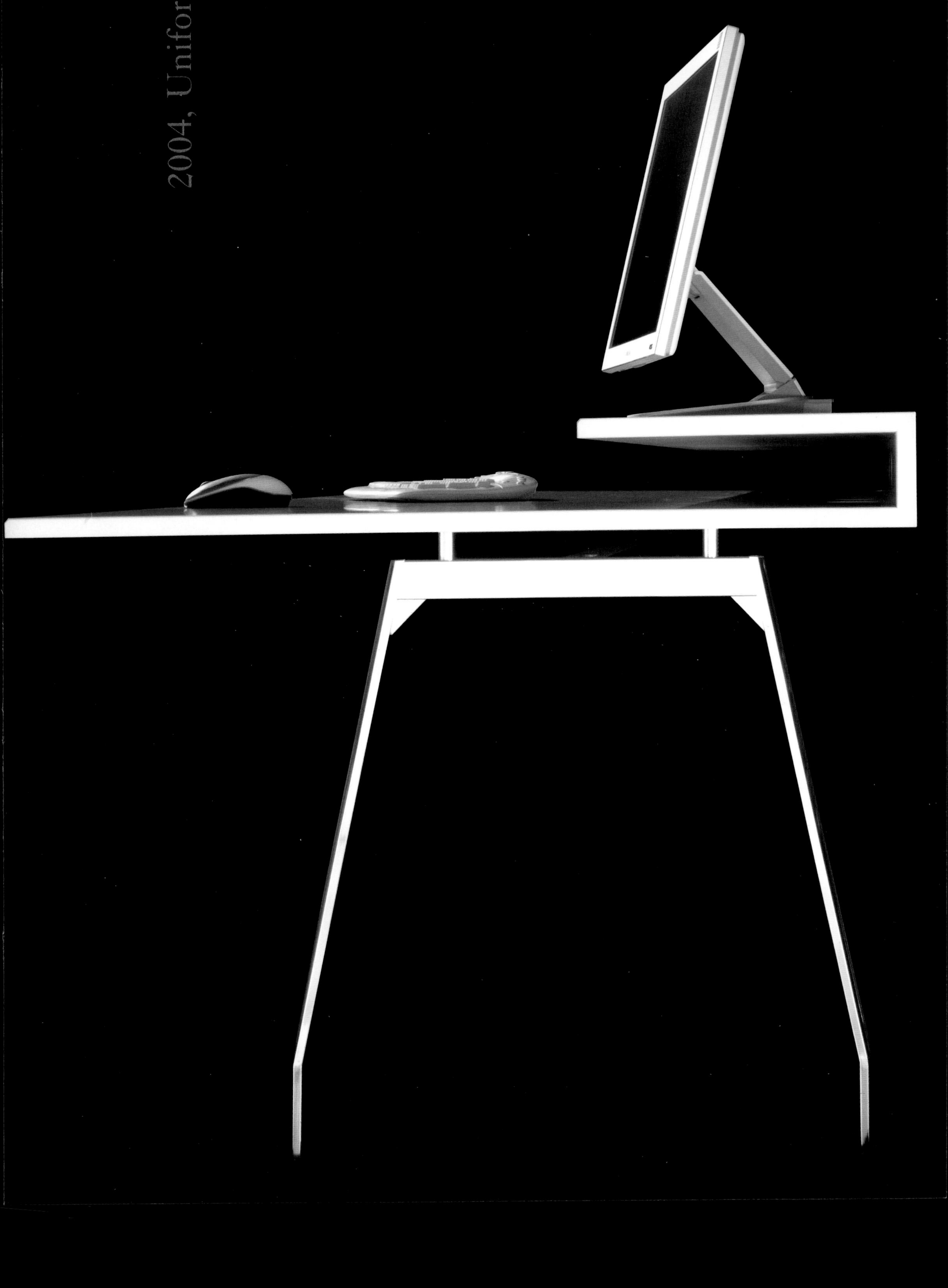

2004, Unifor

Stefano Giovannoni

A rchitect (La Spezia, 1954), founded the King Kong studio with Guido Venturini. Since 1988 he has worked for Alessi. He created a collection of playful, colorful, fairytale and very characteristic objects, based on strong communication elements. The expressive reference world is that of pop, expressing friendly and cosy solutions in numerous objects for the home. These are wide distribution designs sometimes tending toward the sphere of "gadgets."

Mr and Mrs Chin salt and pepper set, 2008, Alessi.

Lilliput
Salt and
Pepper Set

1993, Alessi

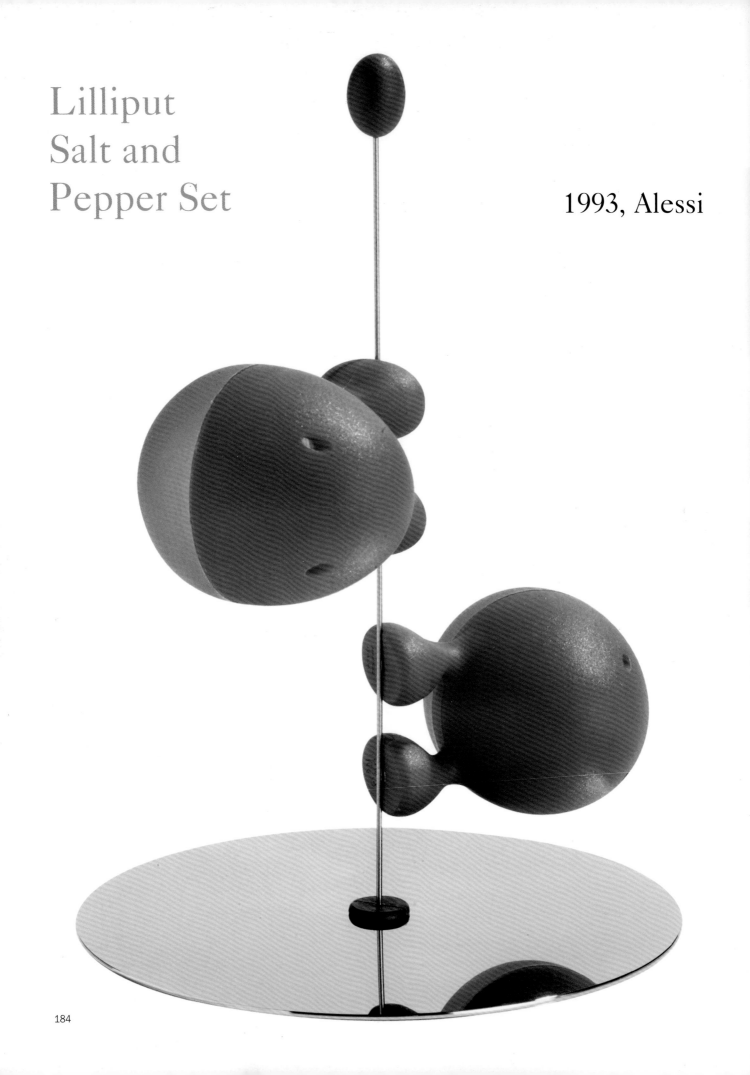

Girotondo
Collection

1994, Alessi

1997, Magis

Alessi Phone
Telephone

2009, Alessi

Giorgetto
Giugiaro

Technical designer (Garessio, 1938), began working when very young as an automobile designer in the Turin Fiat factory, Bertone, Ghia. In 1968 he founded Italdesign, a company which supplied the automobile industry with designs, prototypes, testing and consulting. He is a prolific designer, and under the name Giugiaro Design, founded in 1981, he created products in the most disparate sectors: from furniture to technological objects, from sailing to transport. He has received an honorary degree in Industrial design, three Compasso d'Oro awards, as well as international recognition.

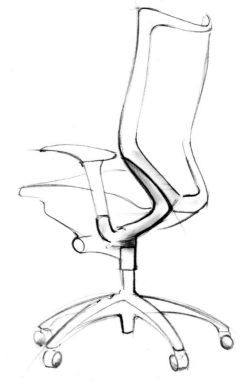

Baron Chair, 2006, Okamura.

Camera
Nikon F3

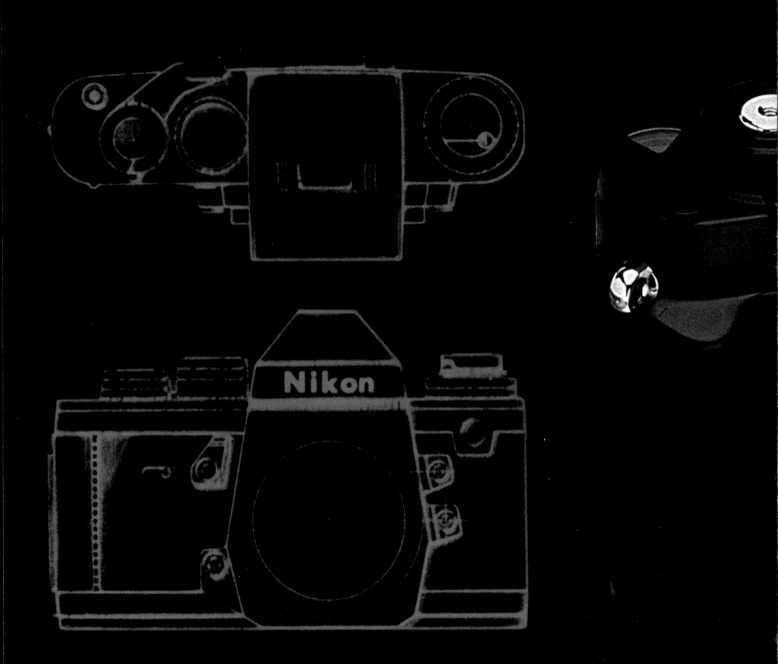

1977, Nikon

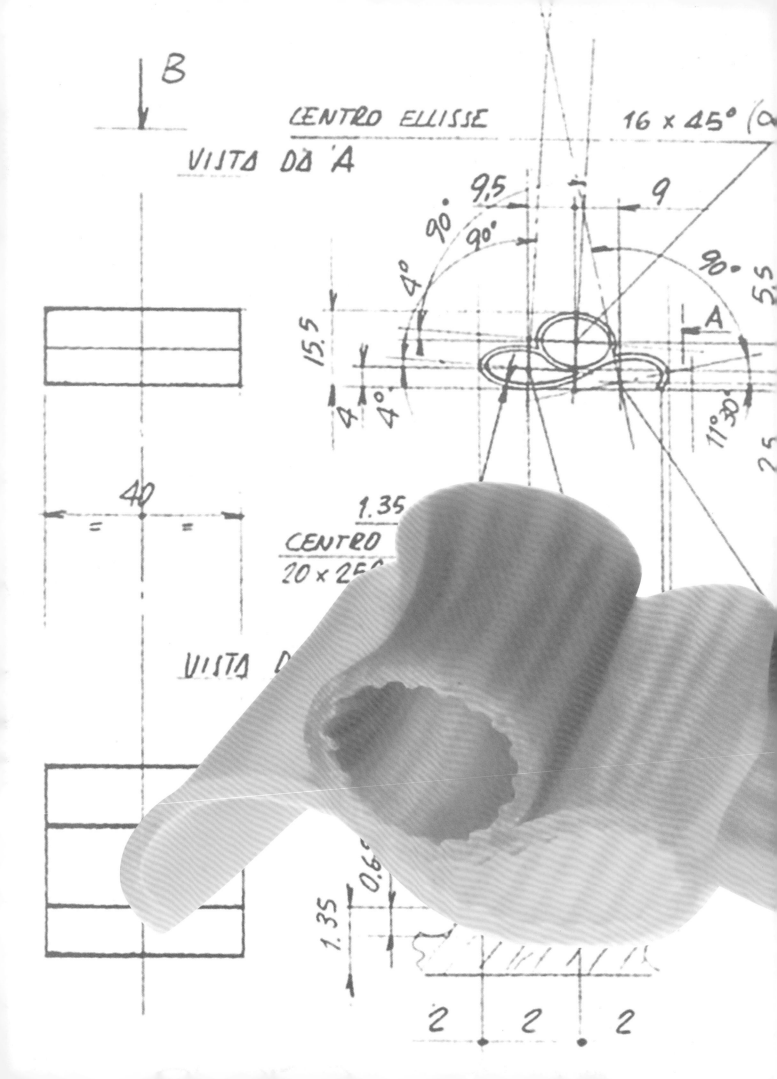

B

CENTRO ELLISSE

VISTA DA 'A

16 × 45° (a

90° 9,5

90°

4° 9

90°

5,5

15,5

A

4°

4°

11°30'

25

1.35

CENTRO

20 × 25

VISTA D

1.35

0,6

2 2 2

Marille Pasta

1983, Voiello

Isotron
Dentist's Chair

1991, Eurodent

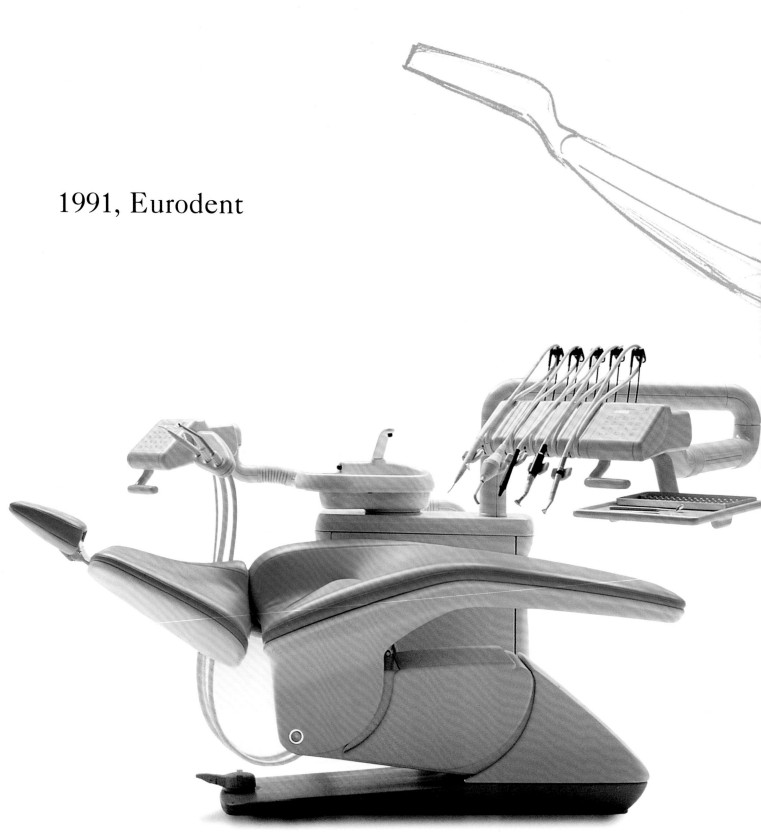

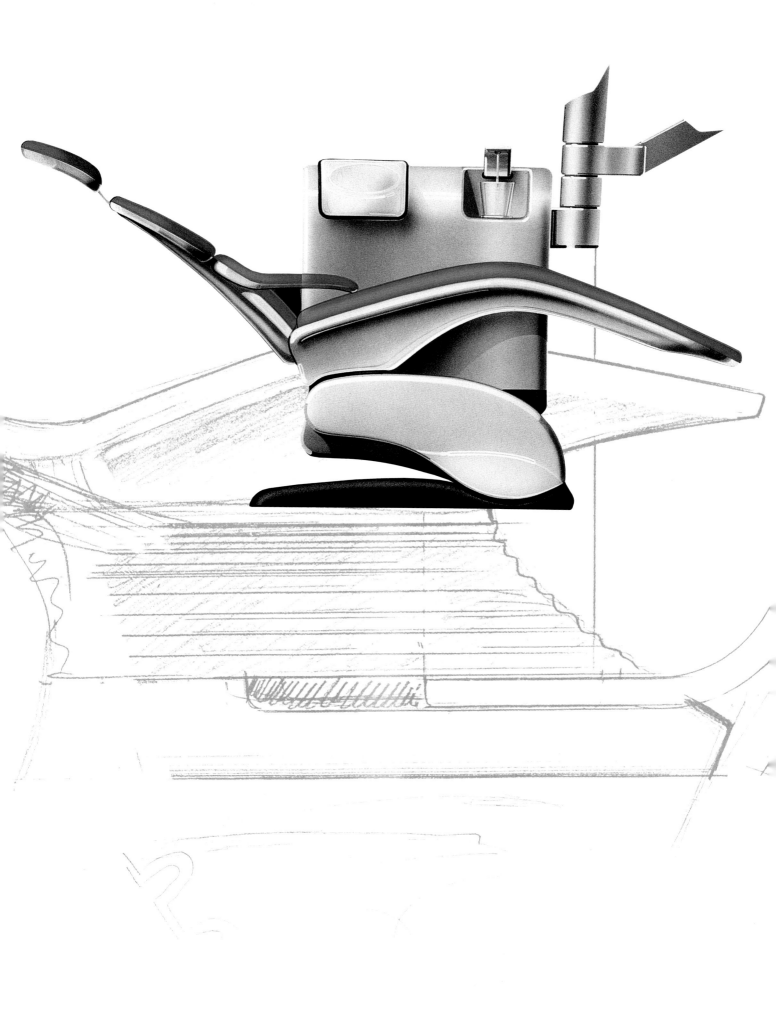

Alberto
Meda

Mechanical engineer (Tremezzina, 1945), from the Seventies onward gained experience with plastics and their manufacture, working with important companies in different sectors, from furnishings to automobiles, to lighting. He worked as an industrial designer, having a strong technological experience and aesthetic sensitivity which he expressed in a soft but incisive fashion. He has received two Compasso d'Oro awards and international recognition. He also teaches and is involved in research.

196 Meda Chair, 1996, Vitra.
197 Teak Collection, 2008, Alias.

Fortebraccio
Lamp

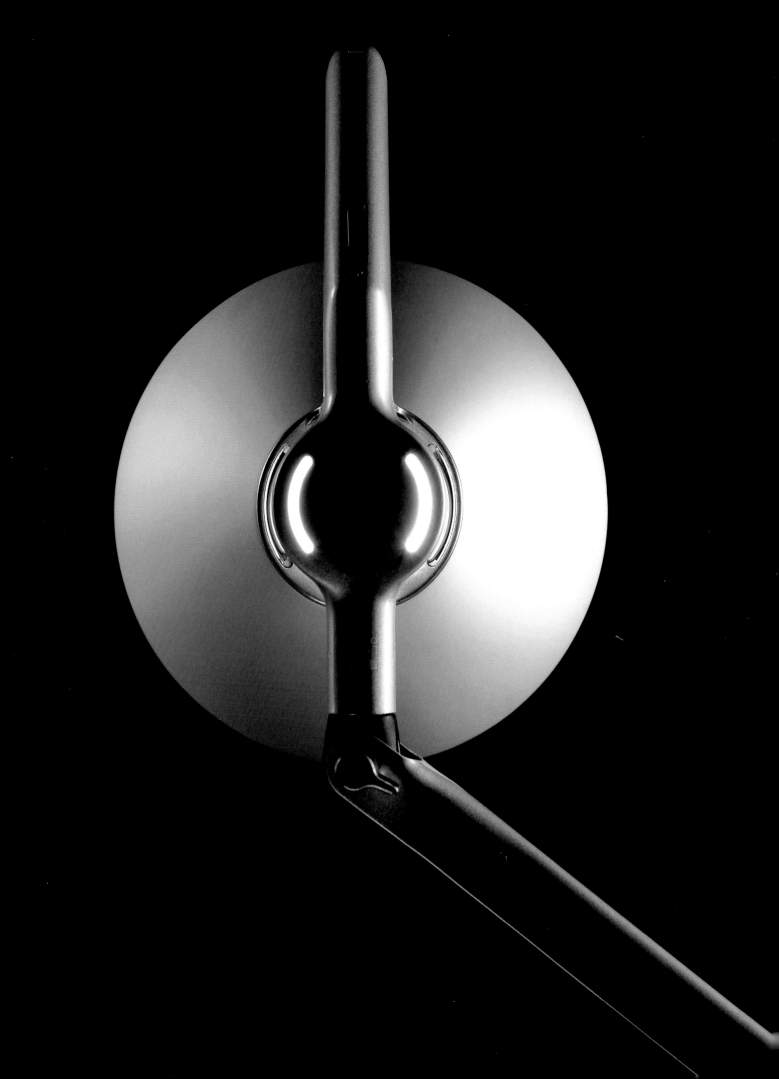

Upper Folding / Step Ladder

2001, Kartell

Fabio
Novembre

Architect (Lecce, 1966), skipped the tortuous rise from the ranks by making himself known as somebody with creative talent and a skilled communicator. He came into the international limelight thanks to some pieces of stage design and designed visionary interiors for fashion shops and showrooms, which made him famous. An artistic and unconventional image is constant in his works.

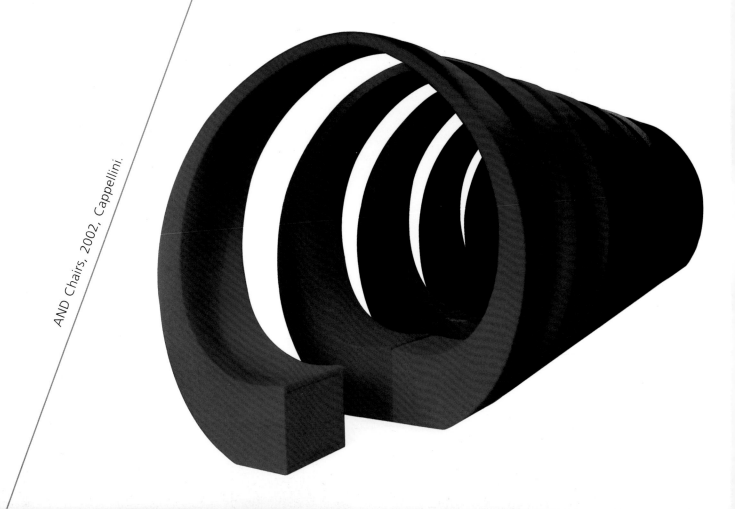

AND Chairs, 2002, Cappellini.

AND Chair
2002, Cappellini

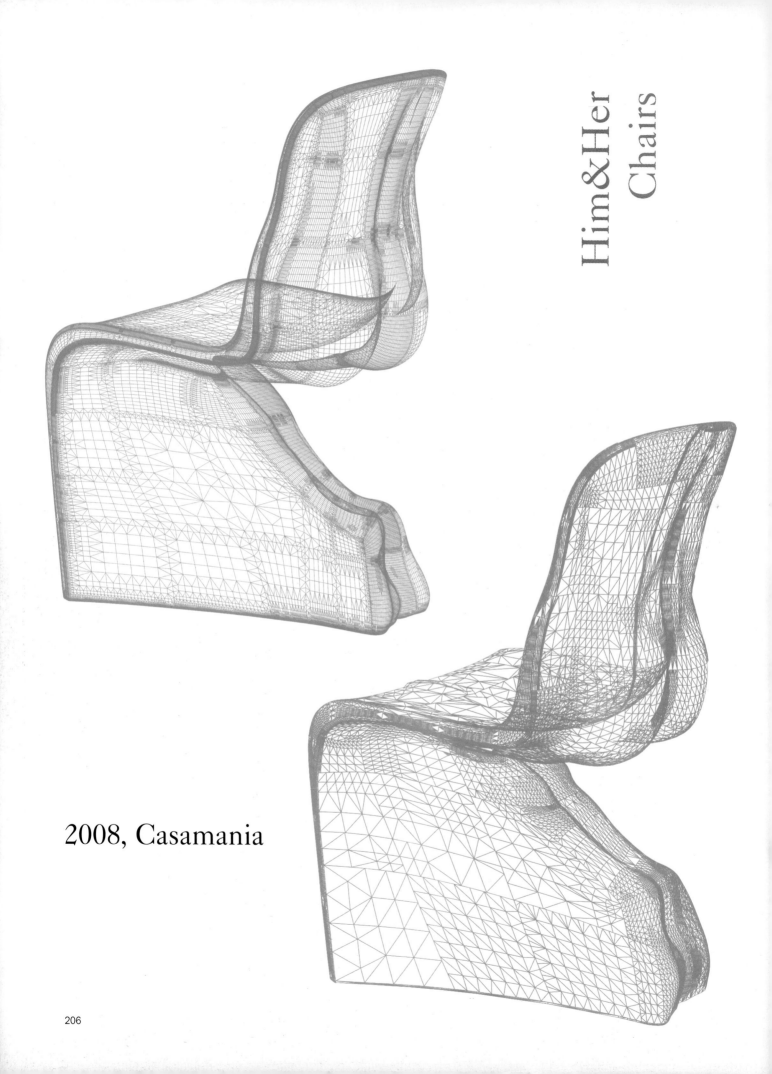

2008, Casamania

Gabriele Pezzini

Designer (Charleroi, Belgium, 1963), tenacious and reflective, analytical and passionate in pursuing his own designs, is a figure of some depth among emerging designers. Supported by an iron will to succeed his profession; at the beginning he gathered a collection of objects and furnishings, including those created by other designers, which he put on sale online. Today he works with various companies, even abroad, on various aspects of design.

Washing Gloves, kitchen gloves, 2005, concept for COOP.

Wired
Chair

2003
Maxdesign

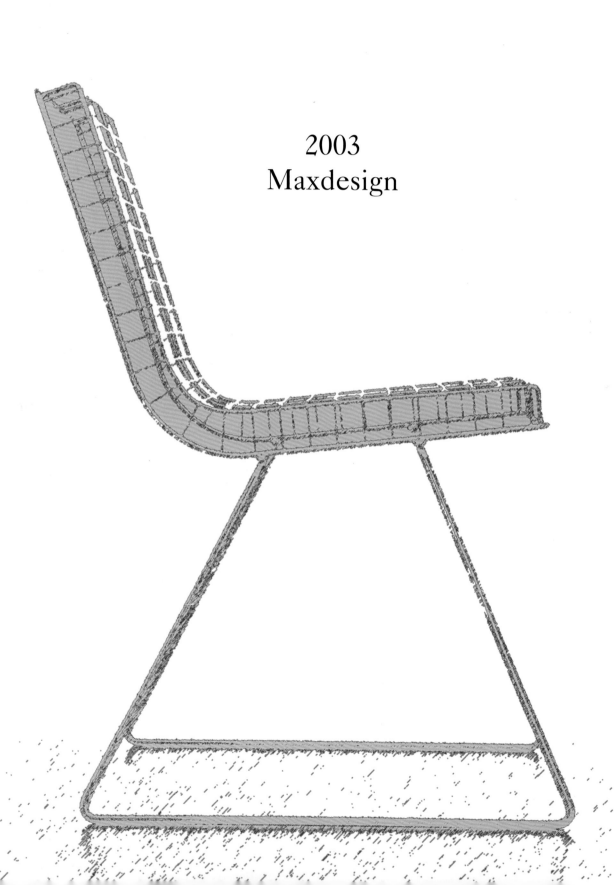

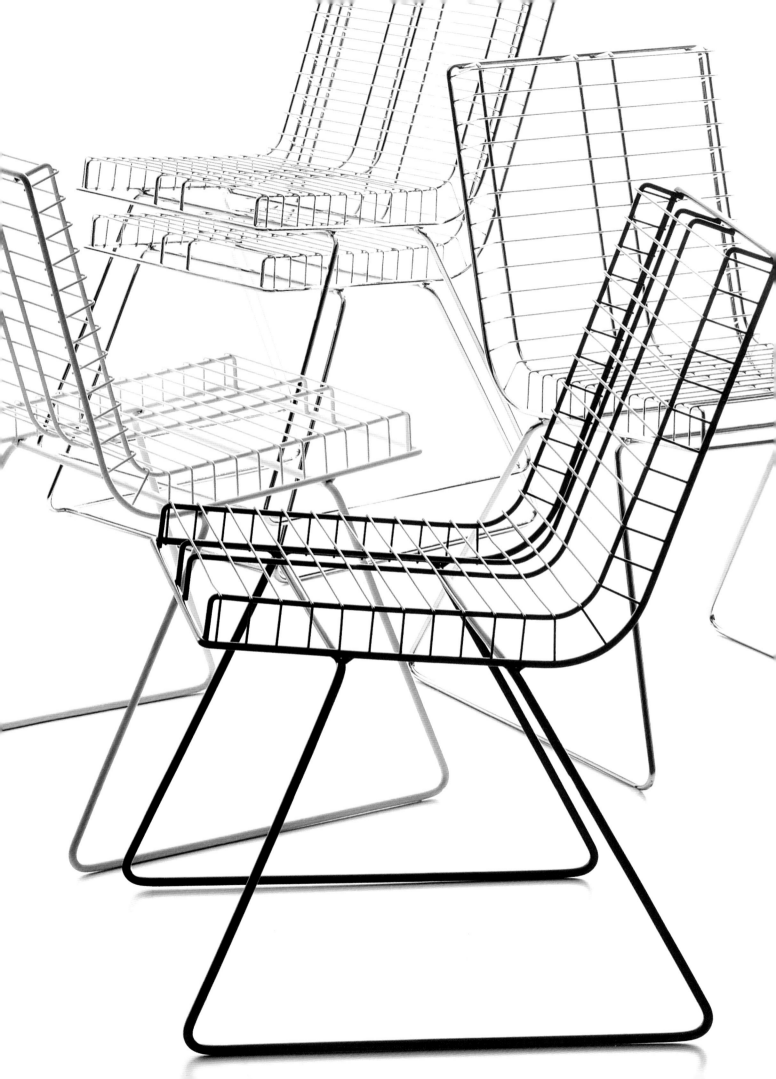

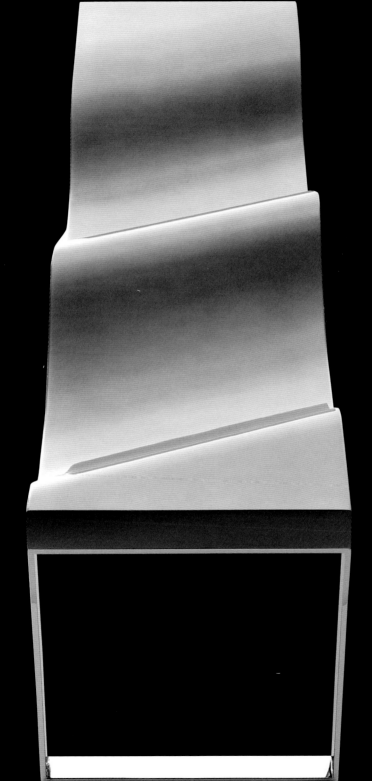

Stripe Chair

Matteo
Ragni

Architect (Milan, 1972), became famous for creating a small bio-degradable multi-purpose piece of cutlery with Giulio Iacchetti, which won the Compasso d'Oro award in 2001. Pragmatic and passionate explorer of new areas of design, capable of identifying, in the humblest everyday object, a potential protagonist, to be seen through new eyes and re-designed with new functionality.

Moscardino Cutlery, 2000,
by Giulio Iacchetti, Pandora Design.

Leti / Lamp

2007, Danese

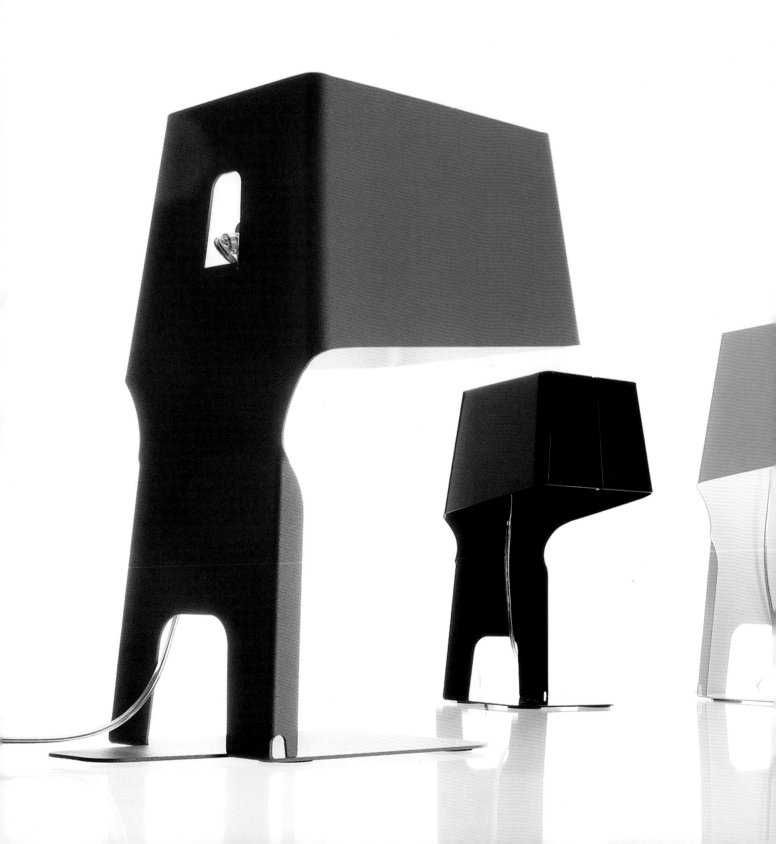

Patch
Book-Ends

2004, De Vecchi

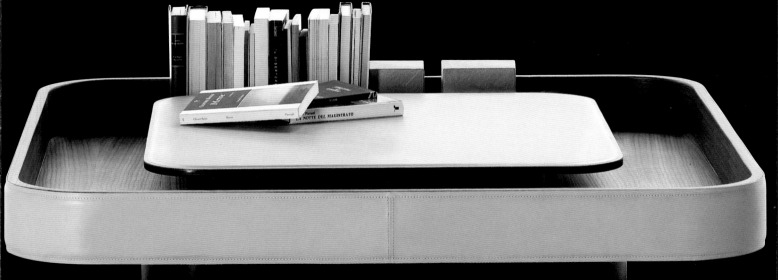

ToBeUs Toy

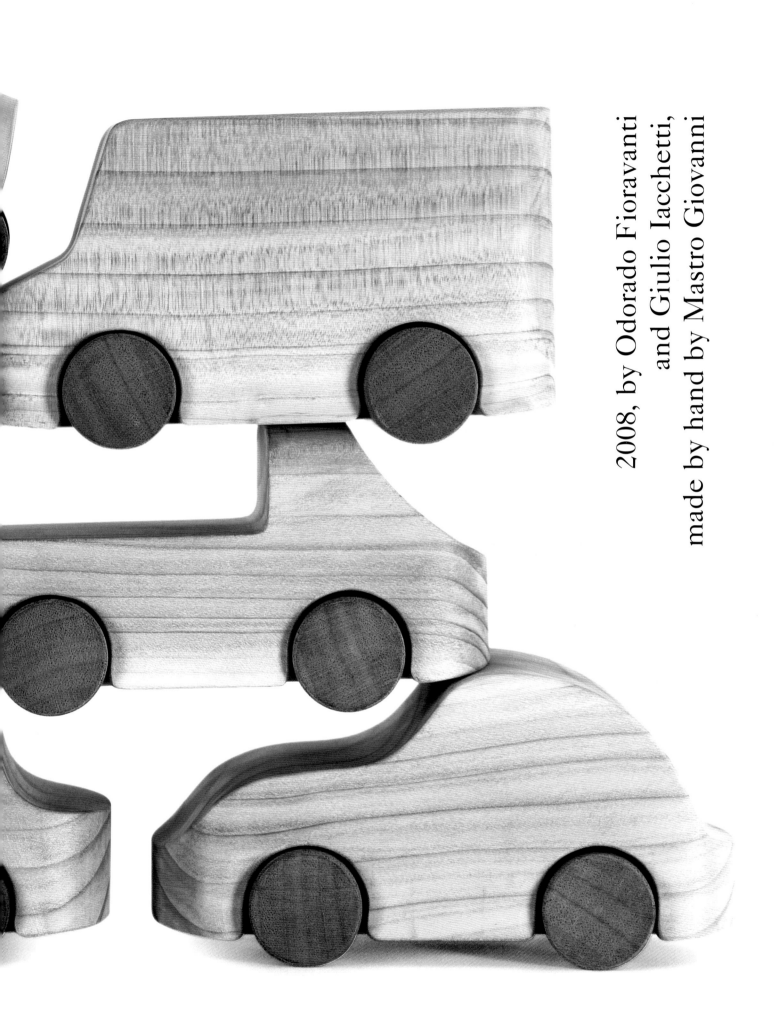

2008, by Odorado Fioravanti
and Giulio Iacchetti,
made by hand by Mastro Giovanni

the adopted ones

While it has been some time now that a few foreign designers have started to move to Italy for work – Makio Hasuike, Bob Noorda, Isao Hosoe, and George Sowden are only a few examples – today the number of designers with studios in Milan has grown dramatically. Young professionals choose the country where it seems simpler to find a company that is capable of converting their ideas and research into reality, young people who are attracted by the world of industrial design schools or by the apparently easy success of a profession which is now considered fashionable. A call which catalyzes figures from all parts of the world and which gives the Italian design scene an international aura, of exchange and métissage. An exchange which today also works in the opposite sense: in fact there are now many Italian companies that use foreign designers and the number of foreign protagonists that can be considered to have been "adopted" by the Italian design scene is constantly increasing. Individuals of different origins and experience who are capable with their very distinctive mark of bringing innovation, generating fashions and trends. And sometimes they succeed in taking the upper hand in numbers over local designers in the catalogues of the more famous companies.

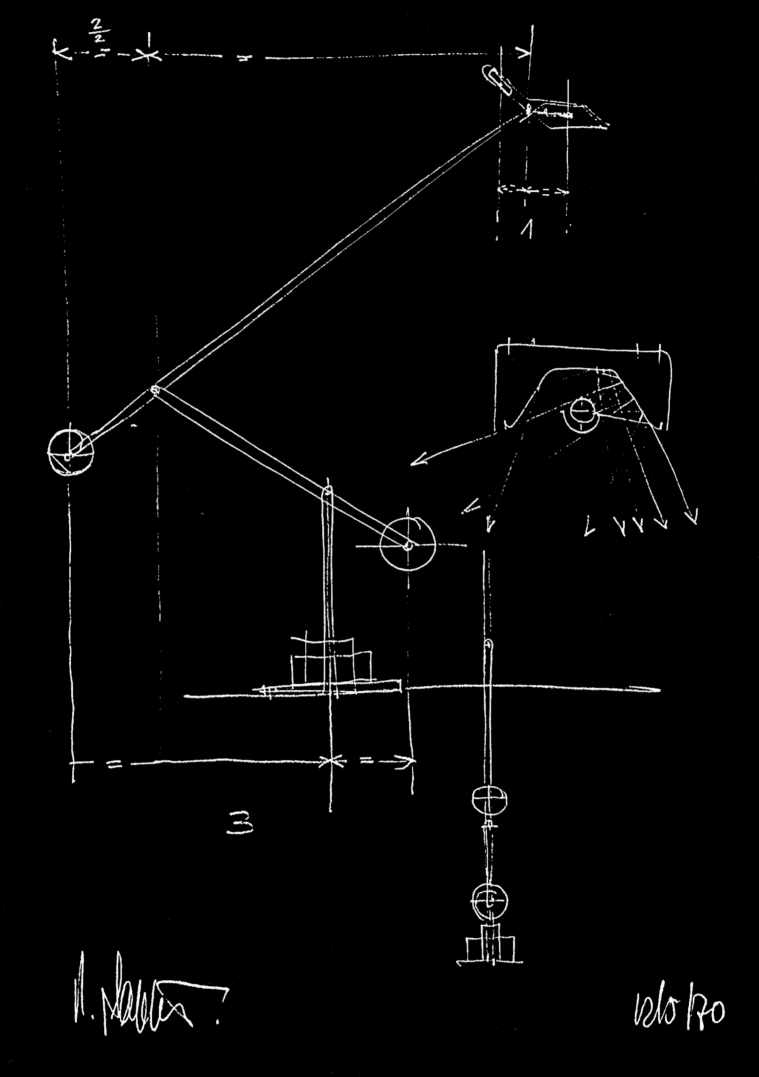

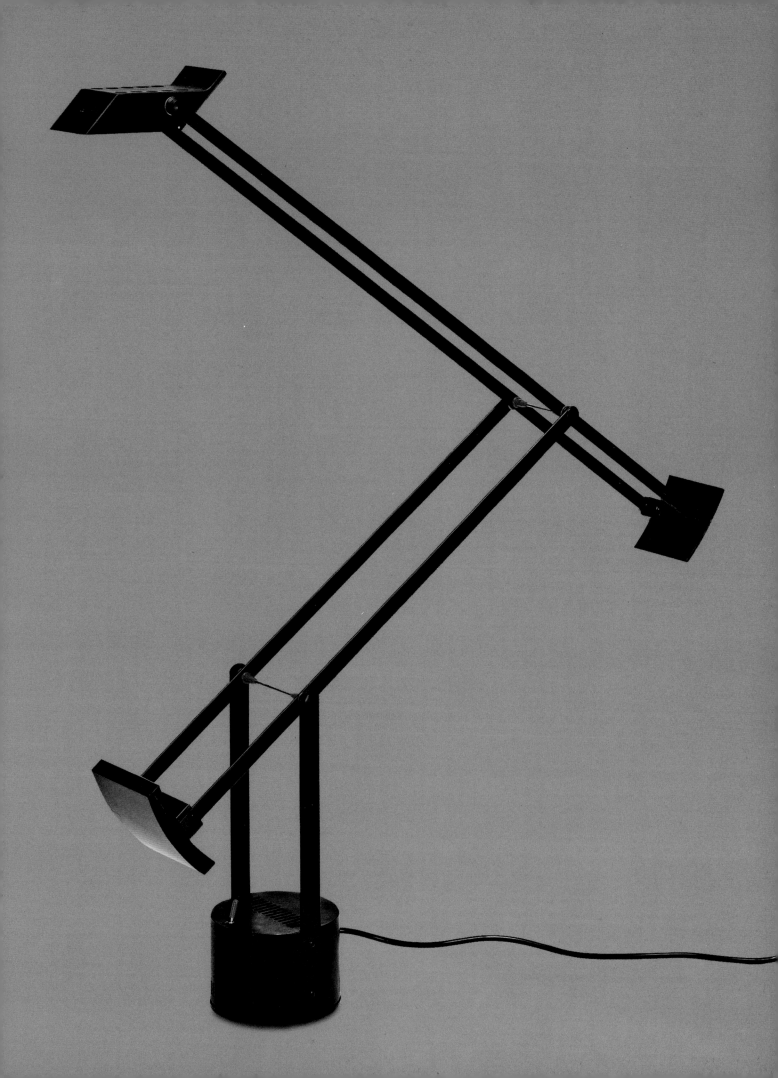

Ron
Arad

Self-taught designer (Tel Aviv, 1951), he moved to London when he was just over twenty and founded One Off, a sort of laboratory/workshop in which he experimented with the first voluminous steel sofas, very similar to works of art, and where the first metallic version of the famous Bookworm bookcase was born. In 1989 he founded Ron Arad Associates, an architecture and design studio, one of the few with an Italian technical branch to take care of the development of the numerous projects with companies in Italy.

Victoria and Albert Armchairs, 2002, Moroso.

Bookworm / Bookcase

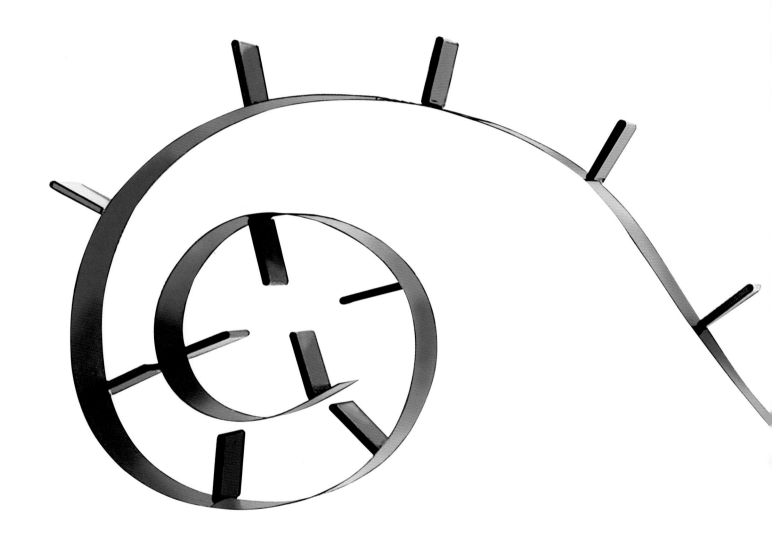

1995
Kartell

231

Ripple Chair

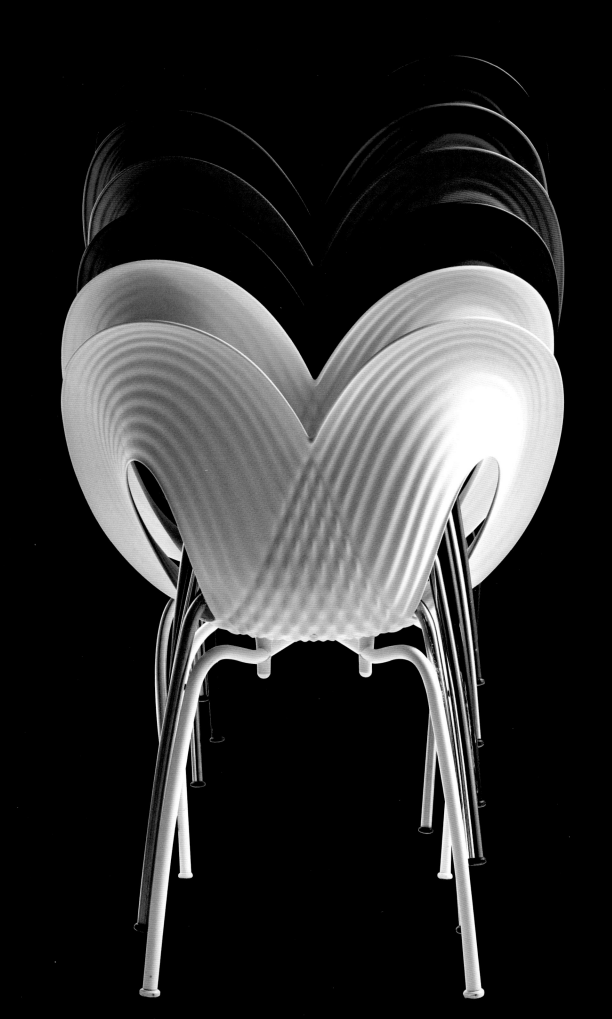

PizzaKobra
Lamp

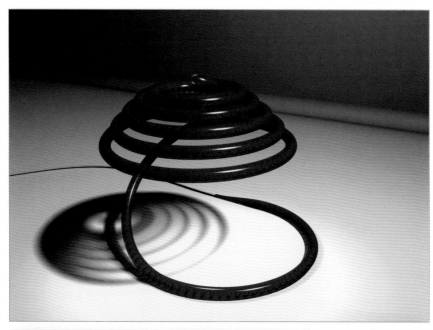

2007, iGuzzini

Fernando
e Humberto
Campana

Discovered by Italian production, they became true icons of Italo-South American design. The two brothers have transformed their innate passion for industrial design into a profession. Humberto (Rio Claro, 1953) graduated in Law whereas Fernando (Brotas, 1961) is an Architecture graduate. Their work is symbolized by a lively and colorful appearance which is derived from the landscapes of the Brazilian favelas, translated into objects which exploit apparently scrap or recycled materials.

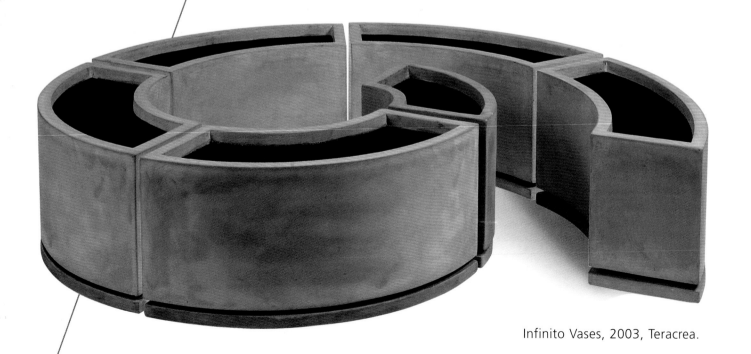

Infinito Vases, 2003, Teracrea.

Vermelha / Chair

2002, Edra

Favela / Chair

2003, Edra

Blow-Up
Basket

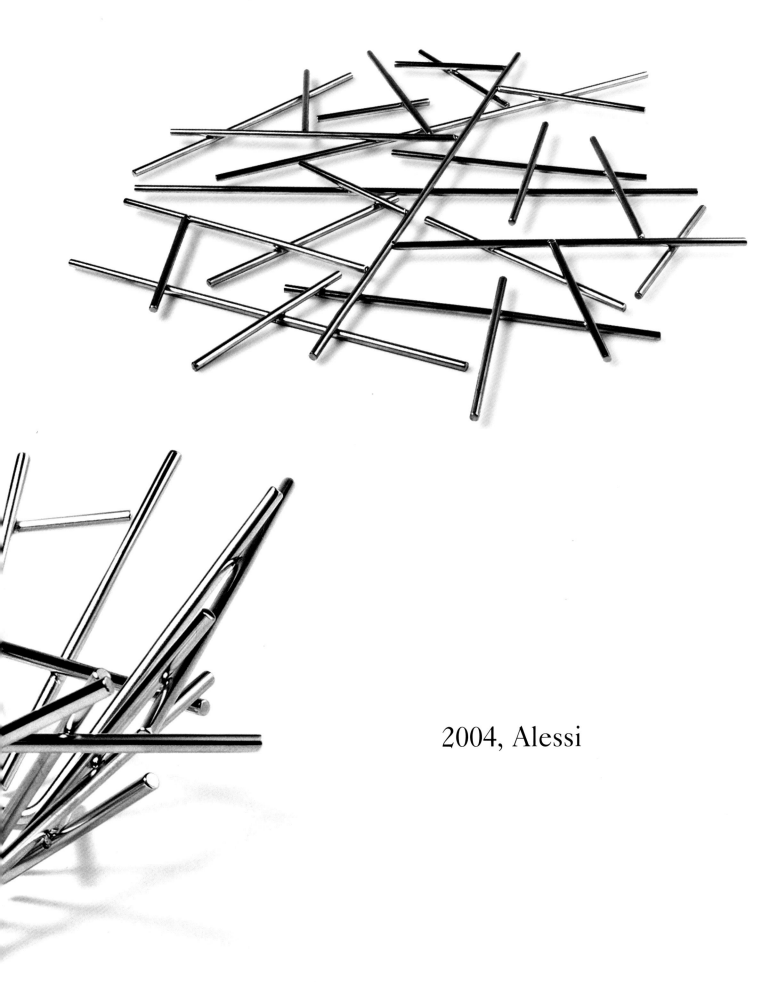

2004, Alessi

Konstantin Grcic

Industrial designer but also a qualified cabinet maker (Munich, 1965) studied at the Royal College of Arts in London and in 1991 he opened the KGID-Konstantin Grcic Industrial Design Studio in his home city. His Mayday lamp won the Compasso d'Oro award in 2001 (and was included in the MoMA collection in New York), a success which introduced him, once and for all, into the élite of the most appreciated designers in Italy. A lover of simple but expressive and ingenious objects, he works for some of the most important companies on various projects, both small and large scale.

Chair One, 2003, Magis.

May Day / Lamp

2000, Flos

Myto Chair

2008, Plank

Jean-Marie Massaud

Designer (Toulouse, 1966), obtained a diploma in Paris at Les Ateliers-EN-SCI. After his early success in France, he is today enjoying a period of fame and recognition even in Italy, thanks to his work with some of the most prestigious producers of furnishings. Basically essential and elegant, giving special attention to the various human needs, he applies himself to different areas of design, moving nonchalantly from furnishing items to the graphics of coordinated images, from interior decoration to architecture.

Seven Table, 2008, B&B Italia.

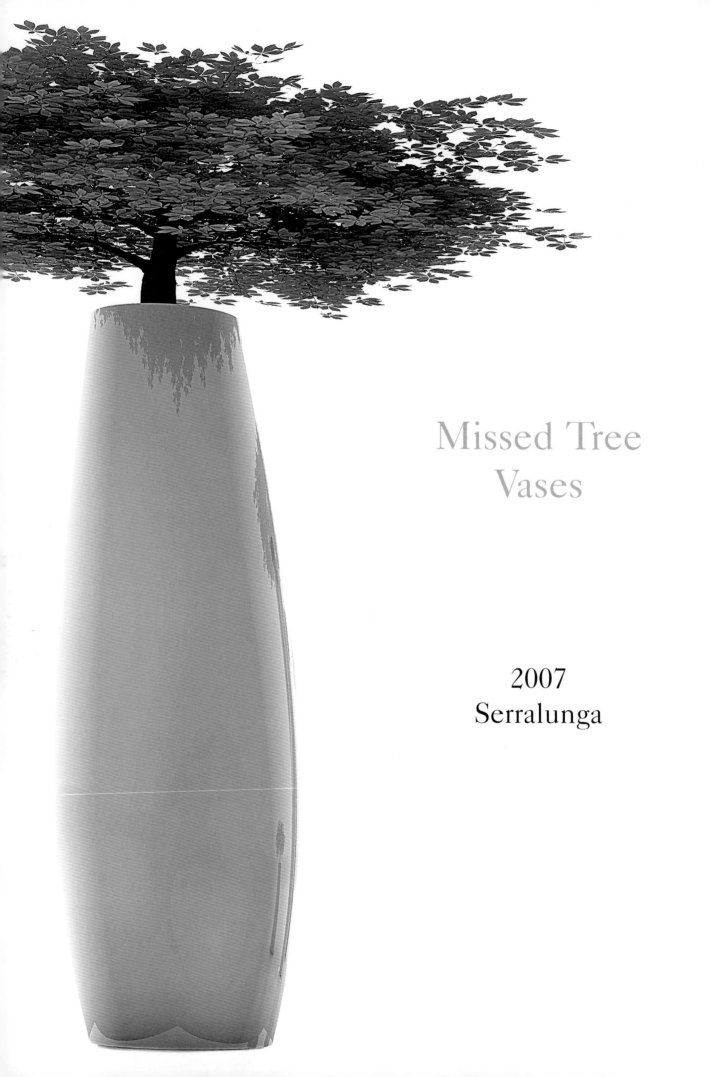

Missed Tree
Vases

2007
Serralunga

Isidoro Trunk-Mobile Bar
2007, Poltrona Frau

Philippe
Starck

Self-taught designer (Paris, 1949), probably owes his Italian success, and not only this, to his Juicy Salif lemon squeezer, a design which is as beautiful as it is almost completely useless. His design strategy changed over the years but not the mark of his decisive characterization. His is a highly rated signature which is very much in demand by corporates in Italy that choose him even to liven up public interiors with some irony and imagination. Currently he is one of those designers that exercise most care for the environment and so as not to empty a beautiful shape of its contents.

Juicy Salif Citrus Squeezer, 1990, Alessi.

Gnomes Table-Stools

La Marie Chair

1998, Kartell

Patricia Urquiola

Architect (Oviedo, 1961), graduated at the Polytechnic in Milan (the city where she has chosen to live and work) with Achille Castiglioni who, together with Vico Magistretti, have been her reference master figures from the beginning of her career. Her creations, which have won multiple awards, characterized by a certain "feminine" spirit, as well as by a contemporary re-reading of traditional techniques and materials, are present in the catalogues of the most renowned Italian lighting and furniture companies.

Flo Chair, 2004, Driade.

Bague / Lamp

2003, Foscarini

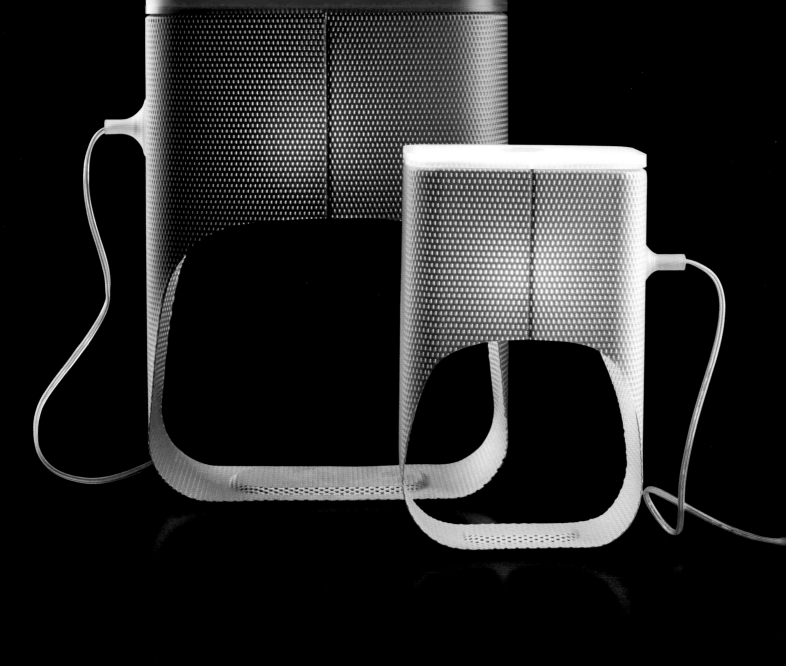

Antibodi
Dormeuse

2006, Moroso

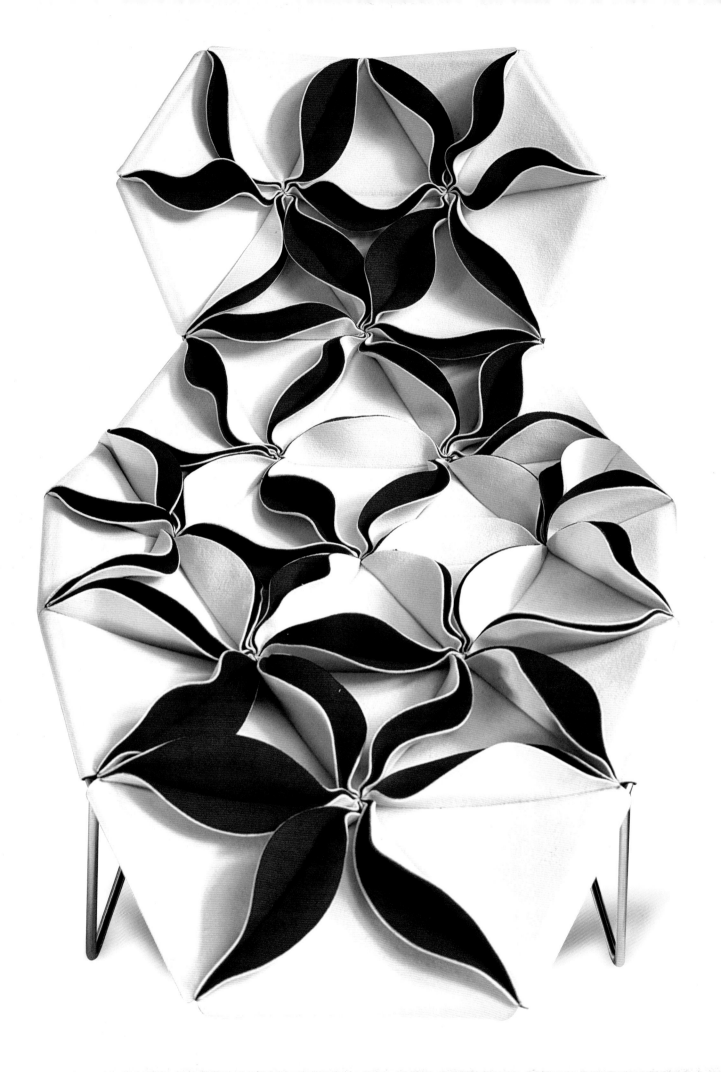

Canasta / Chair

2007
B&B Italia

Index

c = caption
bold = dedicated chapter

Photo
credits

WHITE STAR PUBLISHERS

WS White Star Publishers® is a registered trademark
property of Edizioni White Star s.r.l.

© 2011 Edizioni White Star s.r.l.
Via Candido Sassone, 24 - 13100 Vercelli, Italy
www.whitestar.it

Translation: Catherine Howard
Editing: Peter Skinner

ISBN 978-88-544-0584-4

1 2 3 4 5 6   15 14 13 12 11

Printed in China